Your Soul's Calling

Answering the Question "Why Am I Here?"

BY NANCY CANNING, M.A.

Blessings, Nancy

Canning, Nancy
Your soul's calling: answering the question "why am I here?" / Nancy Canning, M.A. – 1st ed.

ISBN: Paperback: 978-0-9823661-4-1
ISBN: Ebook: 978-0-9823661-5-8
    1. Mind, body and spirit   2. Afterlife   3. Reincarnation

1st edition, November 2015

10 9 8 7 6 5 4 3 2 1

Printed in the United States of America

With deep love and gratitude for my family,

Dick and Peggy Canning,

Barbara, Art, Susan and Bob

Acknowledgements

This book wouldn't have come into physical manifestation without my personal "village," to whom I am deeply grateful:

- To my sister, Barbara McNurlin, for your loving and consistent editorial help, for believing in me and my work, and for keeping me on track.
- To Bob Olson, my friend and colleague, for all your valuable support through the years.
- To my loving friends and colleagues who gave me such insightful feedback and suggestions: Rita Ramsay, Sue McClanahan, and Pashmina Kaur Kohli.
- To my mastermind leader and transformational coach, Felicia Searcy, and the women in the group, Laney, Nea, Rae, Amanda, and Lisa. The consistency of our coaching calls has kept me motivated and helped me through to this finished product.
- To Christy Tryhus and the coaching group in the Mission Marketing Mentors program who inspired me with your own book creations.
- To Hobie Hobart and Kathi Dunn of Dunn-Design.com who created my beautiful cover. What a joy it was to work with you. And to Rochelle Mensidor, for your outstanding layout expertise.
- To Amy Marino at the Sanctuary – Healing Therapies and Gifts, for your beautiful space and ongoing support of my workshops.
- To my incredible friends. You have encouraged me through all your love, your kind words, and your never-ending support.

- To Dr. Brian Weiss, Dr. Michael Newton, John Holland, James Van Praagh, John Edward, Dr. Eben Alexander, and all the other pioneers who led the way to bring past lives and the afterlife into the mainstream.

- And last but by no means least, to all of you who helped me through the ups and downs of listening to my own soul's calling: Dr. Kim Jobst, Dr. John Demartini, Caroline Myss, and the many other spiritual teachers, healers, therapists, and energy workers over the years who have helped me become the woman I am today. Thank you for following your own soul's calling to teach, lead, heal, and transform the world in your own unique ways.

Foreword

For the first 35 years of my life, I had no interest in spirituality. It wasn't until my father died in 1997 that I began to contemplate the deeper questions about life and death. Why are we here? What is my purpose? Where do we go when we die? And why do bad things happen to good people? These are all questions that most of us have asked ourselves. And it was my father's passing that became the catalyst for this personal inquiry, which is a common theme in many people's lives – a loved one's death sparks their spiritual journey.

Being a private investigator by profession, I decided to use my skills as a private eye to find the answers I was seeking. I focused on the afterlife, believing that if I could understand life after death then I would be more likely to gain the bigger answers about purpose and truth as well.

My first evidence of life after death came after stumbling upon a medium, someone who can communicate with people in spirit. My reading was like a reunion between myself and my father, grandmother and several other relatives who are on the other side of life. Since this medium was a stranger to me, who knew details about my life she could not have known but for communicating with my loved ones in spirit, this experience was eye opening. It taught me that there are aspects of life and death of which I was unaware. And I knew that this was the beginning of my awakening.

Once I had experienced mediumship multiple times, I found myself wondering what other experiences were available to me. What's next? I pondered. What other experiences might give me a new level of spiritual insight? I opened our local mind-body-spirit magazine to find a photograph of Nancy Canning smiling at me. I was looking at her 3-inch by 5-inch advertisement for past-life regression and life-between-lives regression. I was drawn to it, so I immediately contacted Nancy and booked a session.

I had no idea just how momentous this experience was going to be for me. To be honest, I didn't really believe I could be regressed. I had heard enough stories to believe other people where regressable (if I can make up a word), but I also knew that my experience as a private investigator led me to maintain control at all times for safety's sake. Nevertheless, I made the 3-hour drive to Cape Cod, and hours after my arrival I left Nancy's office a profoundly changed man. My life would never be the same.

I was so pumped about my remarkable regression experience that I was now extremely eager to consume new experiences. I practiced meditation. I implemented a daily inspired-writing exercise. I had readings with channelers and animal communicators. I consciously and deliberately recorded the signs and signals from spirits known as after-death communications. I had sessions with astrologers, shamans and energy healers. I got a spirit-portrait drawn of my great, great, grandfather by a spirit artist. If there was a new experience to be had, I was signing up for it. And I learned something from each and every one of them. I learned about the experience itself. I learned universal wisdom and truth. And I learned about myself.

Today, more than 18 years since my father's passing, I recognize that this investigation of mine was not just a means to an end; it was my life purpose. Yes I am an investigator, but I am also a teacher – I teach others about my investigations and the conclusions I've drawn based on them. I've written a book about the afterlife, numerous articles about spirituality, created an online show called Afterlife TV, and I have two resources to connect the public with legitimate and reputable psychics, mediums and related practitioners. Who knew my father's passing was going to lead to all this?

Life purpose, consequently, seems to be easier to find than most people realize, because it tends to find us. Your purpose is whatever you are drawn toward. Purpose is not about career unless you want it to be. Some people's purpose in life is to serve as an inspiring example to others, or to be kind to whomever crosses their path in any given day, or to express courage in spite of their challenging circumstances, or to nurture people and animals as if they were all their children.

I learned that we are here simply to have experiences that we as souls are unable to have in the loving, safe light of the spirit world (our true home). So we come here to this earthly life where love exists, but only as an option from which we can choose. We also have options that teach us about love by showing us the opposite, such as hatred, greed, fear, and separation. These free-will choices set the stage for some very interesting, albeit challenging and painful, experiences. It seems that the more we choose love in life, the more pleasurable life tends to be for us.

Along my journey, I discovered there are spiritual experiences that I am unable to schedule with a practitioner or practice in my home. One example is having a near-death experience. This is one of the most fascinating experiences in the afterlife arena, but it is something that happens to people unpredictably and uncontrollably. And, of course, not everyone who dies for a few seconds or minutes and then recovers back to life has a near-death experience. So rather than experience this for myself, I conducted extensive interviews with people who have had NDEs.

During my research of near-death experiences, I noticed that I was able to relate to what these near-death experiencers were describing. How could this be? I wondered. And then I realized that the feelings they had during their NDE, the way they felt out of their body and in the spirit world, even the way they communicated telepathically, were all experiences I had known during my past-life and life-between-lives regressions. Yes, of course! I too was out of my body and in another dimension during these regressions. I got enthusiastic about the similarities between the two experiences. It helped me to understand these NDEs that most near-death experiencers say are difficult to put into words.

There is one other fundamental result of having spiritual experiences that I noticed yet hear few people mention. When we have any of these experiences that I've discussed thus far, particularly the regression experiences, we gain a 'knowing' about spiritual truth that seemingly satiates us as an unexpected and often unnoticed consequence of the experience itself. Said another way, we seem to absorb wisdom while having the experience. More interestingly, this absorbed wisdom appears to bypass our intellect and lies dormant within us until, one day, we surprisingly find ourselves acting with greater patience, compassion, love and fearlessness in the face of challenges that would have previously shaken us off our rails and had us acting with less desirable qualities.

Accordingly, spiritual experiences of any kind have an exponential effect on us that is so much more than the stages that unfolded or the stories about them that we later share with others. We learn lessons, of course, but we also raise our vibration – individually and collectively. Our physical energy moves away from the frequency of fear and closer to the frequency of love. Moreover, we accept and appreciate our connection to our higher self, whatever term you give it, so that we learn to trust the guidance that flows in our life. In this way, we listen to our intuition and pay attention to the coincidences and messengers in our life.

I can tell you for sure that I was not seeking or expecting this result when I underwent the various sessions and practices I chose for experiment. Instead, I unwittingly became a more loving, authentic, empathetic, patient and understanding human being than I was before my investigation into life after death. Naturally, just like everyone, I still have a long way to go, since personal and spiritual growth are ongoing processes. But I trust fully that everyone, including myself, is exactly where we are supposed to be at this moment in time, which prevents me from wanting to control people and circumstances out of fear that someone or something is heading in a challenging direction. And that gives me a sense of inner peace that was once rare or nonexistent in my life.

Today I teach more and seek new experiences less, but in hindsight I realize that out of all the experiences I have known, my past-life and life-between-lives regressions held the most impact on my spiritual growth. This is because they are personal experiences. Someone wasn't telling me what my past life was like; I was reliving it myself. And that distinction between personal experience and secondhand knowledge makes all the difference, because only personal experience can lead us to 'knowing.'

Nancy Canning gave me my first past-life and life-between-lives regressions about 15 years ago. She taught me a great deal at the beginning of my journey, and her work has helped me to recognize my own soul's calling. Now, 15 years later, she has taken the wisdom she's gained from working with clients and having her own sacred experiences to help you discover your own soul's purpose for being here. The result is this life-changing manual of life and purpose that I wish was available to me when I still felt lost and wandering without a sense of direction in my life. I am honored and thrilled to be writing the Foreword to such a valuable contribution to spiritual-growth literature. And I'm happy for you that it has come into your awareness.

Whether you are just beginning your spiritual voyage or wanting to build upon years of insight and experience, you can expect many 'Aha!' moments while reading this book. I learned new truths and gained new tools from it, and I was also reminded of knowledge that I had previously learned but somehow forgotten. I have already utilized this book's teachings in unexpected and valuable ways. I hope you share the same experience and allow the teachings within to expand and illuminate your life.

With love,

Bob Olson
Author of *Answers About The Afterlife: A Private Investigator's 15-Year Research Unlocks The Mysteries Of Life After Death* and host of *AfterlifeTV.com*.

October 10, 2015

Contents

1

Two Thumbs Up

"We did it! We created the life we wanted!" – Peggy Canning

In September 2010 I was on a plane flying over the desert in Utah or Nevada, headed for San Francisco. That morning, I had received the call that no one wants to receive: Come home now, Dad is dying. Our mother had died nine months earlier, on New Year's Eve. Dad had been in decline since, so we four siblings knew he was fading.

The previous night I told him on the phone, "Dad, don't hang around for any of us. We don't want you to go, but it's OK when you're ready." I had meant sometime in the future. However, unbeknownst to me, he went into a coma two hours later. My older brother and sister were with him that night, and my younger sister had flown in that morning. I was on my way to Dad as fast as I could get there: a long cross-country journey from Boston to San Diego.

Suddenly, Dad was there with me in the plane. I could hear his voice as plain as day: "I'm sorry, Sweetie, but I couldn't wait any longer." I knew he had just died. His energy was rather scattered and diffuse. In comparison, I could see (energetically and psychically) my mother with him. Her energy was "nicely put together." She'd had time to regain her soul essence and to be healed.

I saw her with two thumbs up, very happy and proud, saying to my father, "We did it! We created the life we wanted!" She was so happy!

I said to myself then, and I continue to say to myself now, "I want that! At the end of this life, I want to give two thumbs up and be happy and proud of my life."

And I want that for you, too. I want to help you create that kind of ending for yourself. That's why I'm writing this book: To help you understand your life from your soul's point-of-view and be able to really hear your soul's calling.

You Are A Time Traveler

While your physical body is limited to being in this time and space, your soul has been traveling throughout time without regard for space. You have lived in other bodies on earth, and, chances are high that you will live on earth again. You have had many bodies, but only one soul, which is uniquely you.

Here's the good news: Your soul has a fabulous memory, far better and more accurate than your brain's memory. It remembers details of your past lives, what you do in between your lives, and even more importantly, the agreements and plans you made for this life.

This book aims to help you understand why things have happened to you in this life as they have, so that you can accept these events and understand your life's purpose.

Know this:

Before coming into this lifetime, your Soul/Higher Self planned what you wanted to learn, experience, and accomplish during your time here on earth. Your soul is calling you to remember your plans.

If you already know this statement is true for you, and you've been searching for your purpose in being alive, then you're already listening to your soul calling to you.

On the other hand, if this statement doesn't ring true for you, or you simply don't understand it, then just by reading this introduction you're listening to your soul. It's calling you to open up and remember who you are. You may put this book down at this point and not read another sentence, and still, this statement has been planted in your consciousness as a way to help you remember who you really are (a spiritual being) and why you are here in your body (to learn and grow).

I am a time-traveler guide. I lead people into other lives they have lived, as well as into the afterlife (our life-between-lives, aka heaven or the spirit world). By so doing, I help people learn about their soul's journey. Even though this book is about your spiritual path, it is practical information. I will show you how you can look at your life and discern the all-important question so many people want answered: "Why am I here?"

I think all of us ask these questions, don't we?

- "Why in the world am I here?"
- "What am I here to learn?
- "Why is this happening to me?"
- "How can I know what my soul wants?"
- "How do I even know what my soul is?"
- "Have I really lived before…and will I live again?"
- "How can I know this is all true and not just made up hocus pocus?"
- "How do I find real meaning and purpose in my life?"

You may have the feeling that something is not quite right or is missing in your life. You know there's more you're meant to do but for the life of you, you can't figure it out. Your life doesn't "add up quite right" because some things have happened that don't make sense. You may know you are far more capable than the way you are showing up.

Or, perhaps your life is comfortable and you are happy in your work or family or creativity. You're not at a crossroads, but rather, life is just going along for you. And yet, you may feel inner nudges. They may be compelling you to question your higher purpose, or wonder about your intuition or guidance. You may even wonder how to communicate with your soul.

Or you may know exactly what you are here to be and do this lifetime, but can't figure out how to make it happen. Perhaps fear is holding you back, or doubt and uncertainty, or even the thought that you need to know a little bit more before you can really live your life purpose.

If any of these situations apply to you, or if this is all gibberish to you, and you don't know what I'm talking about, keep reading. It may begin to make sense to you shortly.

Why Did I Even Get Born?

One of our poignant questions, especially if we're having a difficult time, is "Why did I even get born?" If heaven is so wonderful, why do we leave it to come to earth? Why don't we just stay there? Why do we show up in rough lives?

When things are going well, you may be enjoying the sunrises and sunsets, you're in love, you're creating, you're helping others, and there's enough of everything. You may be thinking, "This is why I came."

But things can get really tough. Sometimes life isn't working for you, and no matter what you do, you can't seem to get out of the struggle. That's when the thought pops up, "I don't understand. Why can't I get it together? Why can't I have the life I want?"

Through the ages, scholars and mystics, prophets and sages have expounded on this conundrum. Here's a brief explanation of what I believe about this very big subject.

Physics is beginning to catch up with religion and spirituality in proving that there is an Essence that is found in everything. A few of the many different terms to describe that Essence are: God, Infinite Intelligence, Source of All That Is, Creator, and Allah. I certainly do not refer to God as some male figure in the sky or some persona that is a human reflection. Rather, God is Light, Love, Consciousness, Creative Source, and Being.

My belief is that God is Love, which means that the Source of All That Is can be nothing other than Love, equally loving at all times, in all places, in all situations.

As an immortal soul, we each are part of this Source of Love. Think of God as the ocean and your soul as a drop of ocean water. You are the same essence as the ocean. You are fully ocean. Yet, you are not the entire ocean. You are the essence of God, Love, and yet you are not all of God. You don't create universes and galaxies, and yet you create your own personal world with your thoughts and actions. You are here to remember the truth that you are One with God and then learn to live from this Truth.

As a soul, we want to grow and evolve into all that we can possibly be. In the spirit world, we are aware of our spiritual nature and the areas in which we want to grow so that we can be more loving, more God-like. It's our innate God nature to want to be Love and be fully who we are. Earth provides us the circumstances to grow because it tests our ability to be Love, always. Even though life on earth is painful at times, as a soul we want to evolve, and being in a human body is our pathway.

In each lifetime, we have lessons to learn, with many facets to each lesson. One lesson, of course, is to be Love. It's not the only lesson, but it's our primary one. We learn different facets of being Love in different lifetimes, including how to not be Love. We need to learn all sides of being Love before we are proficient in giving, receiving, and being loving to ourselves and to all others. Although, as an immortal soul, our nature is to be Love, it takes lifetimes of practice to live this truth in everyday human life. That's what earth school is for.

To explain this using an analogy, you may be gifted with musical talent and read all about how to play the piano. You memorize the notes, keys, and pedals, but until you actually sit down at the keyboard, you aren't playing the piano. Playing the piano is the goal. Mentally studying how to play the piano is part of the process to attain the goal, but it's not the goal itself.

In the same way, the learning we do in the spirit world is part of the process to help us reach our goal of evolving as spiritual beings. Our goal is to incarnate into a physical body and actually live life with all of its conflicts and suffering, as well as its fullness of joy and passion, all the while remembering the truth of our soul essence, remembering to be Love. Living life in our human body is the process through which we spiritually evolve, and this evolution requires living many lifetimes.

I'll start with my own story of how I got into this work of helping people find their life purpose. Throughout this book, I refer to two types of clients' hypnosis sessions that I have conducted to help them better understand their life purpose: past lives and life-between-lives spiritual regressions. I'll briefly describe them both so that you have an idea of what clients experience.

My Story

"This is the life you've been dying to live" is a favorite past life joke of mine.

In 1982 I did not believe in reincarnation. I could take it or leave it, and I actually preferred to leave it. One evening I was talking with friends. I don't remember what we talked about, but I do know it was not about reincarnation or foreign countries.

Suddenly, and spontaneously, I slipped into a past life in Japan. I could see it as clearly as watching a movie in my mind. I knew with every fiber of my being that I was the young girl I saw, with long, straight black hair and a vivid blue blouse. I was about 10 years old, hiding in a ditch with my younger brother. There were Samurai soldiers marching nearby and we were crouched down to keep from being seen by them.

As I watched this "memory movie" unfold in my mind, I was frightened and confused, and began yelling out loud what I was witnessing. I kept saying, "I'm making this up!" But I knew inside that it was very real. I'm very grateful that one of my friends was immediately aware of what I was going through and encouraged me to stay with the experience. It was over fairly quickly, but it shook me to my core. I couldn't dismiss it as imagination because there was a deep knowing inside me that it was much more: It set me on my path.

After that dramatic introduction, I began clairvoyant training to "read" past lives as a psychic. A person would sit in front of me, I would close my eyes and wait for images to appear to me, and then I would tell the person out loud the scene I was seeing, what the person looked like, the action I was being shown, and the life lesson that particular scene represented. I would see scenes from different ages, some normal everyday activities and sometimes traumas or dramatic events. Traumatic deaths tend to remain more energized, so those would often appear.

During the next eight years of intensive psychic work, I "read" hundreds, perhaps over a thousand, past lives. Many readings had profound effects on the clients and helped them on their life's journey.

Early in 1998 I spent an intensive month studying hypno-therapy. In my private therapy practice, I began using hypnosis to lead clients into their own past lives. So rather than me relating to them the stories I psychically saw, I used (and still use) hypnosis to gently assist them in going back to a past life that dealt with an issue they are dealing with in this life. By experiencing another life for themselves, the vast majority of my clients gain three major benefits: (1) They release all fear of death, (2) they validate their immortality, and (3) they understand their current life better.

After so many years and past life experiences, all my doubts and misgivings about believing in and knowing our souls' undying nature have long since given way.

From the hypnosis experiences of clients over the past fifteen years, I have learned a lot about life purpose and lessons. The subject of life purpose and the soul's journey through numerous lives has been a passion of mine for many years. I'm pleased to share some of these fascinating sessions in this book to illustrate different lessons and principles of the soul's journey.

Past Lives

So many people ask: Have we really lived other lives before this one? How do we know? How can we "prove" it?

To answer these questions briefly: I believe we all have lived past lives, and I have helped thousands of people to experience their past lives. I may not prove the reality of past lives to you, but here's what I have learned about them:

You have been born into this life as a continuation of your soul's journey. All that you have been and done in your former lives has led you to be who you are today.

Therefore, by looking at your present life, you can discern how your past is still affecting you. By looking at your past lives, you can better understand your current life as well as the journeys you have taken through time.

In the end, it is this life, the here and now, that matters most and is where your focus needs to be.

If you don't believe in past lives, or are highly skeptical, keep reading because you can still learn a great deal from these stories. The wisdom and truths these clients gained do not depend on past lives being real. Even if you believe it's all made up, the stories can still be helpful to you.

From a spiritual perspective, you are the sum total of all you have been throughout your incarnations. People often ask, "How many lives do people typically have?" I heard one "expert" on the subject answer, "People can have up to nine lives." Another "expert" said, "You can have over 600,000 lives." So what's the "real" answer? My guess is that it's somewhere between those two numbers.

When a person enters into the spirit world, the number of lives lived is not a question that is asked because it's irrelevant. What's important is not how many lives we've lived but rather the progress our soul has made on its journey and the life lessons we have learned.

We all identify with our current body, personality, gender, and race, so it may be difficult for us to imagine ourselves as a person in another life as the opposite sex, or another race, a different body size and type, or a very different religion or personality.

From all the past lives I have helped my clients explore, I have learned that we don't remain the same gender and race in every lifetime. Yes, we may have a soul preference to be either male or female, but we will still come into some lives as the other gender to learn how to better understand and walk in the shoes of someone different from ourselves. It's also highly likely that you have lived in many different countries, having skin color that was white, black, brown, and all shades in between.

It's quite the experience to go into another lifetime during hypnosis and feel yourself as a very different type of person than who you are now, especially if you change gender and/or race, or have a very different personality. This experience is especially helpful if you hold judgments against other types or races of people, or are sexist and hold the mindset that, of course, your gender is superior. Living through a lifetime that is different than your present one can help you more deeply understand and have compassion for people you previously might not have acknowledged as equal or somehow similar to you.

Underneath the skin color, race, and gender, we are all the same, moving through our life with challenges and successes, giving and receiving love, creating and changing, seeking to be recognized and regarded, and all that encompasses the human experience.

If you are searching for answers to deep questions about your own past lives and reincarnation's validity, I believe you're in for some surprises. Your soul's journey this lifetime may be for you (and your logical mind) to come to terms with your previous lifetimes. The clues about who you have been and where you have lived are all around you. It's usually a journey and a process to learn to trust your inner knowing and let go of your doubts about past lives. Appendix A has more information on evidence about past lives, plus you can visit my website at *www.nancycanning.com* for further resources on this subject that you may find interesting.

We Are All Here in Earth School

When we begin going to school, we're at the start of a new learning adventure. We learn the letters of the alphabet, how to use these letters to make words, and then how to print those letters and words. We learn math, how to add and subtract in very simple ways. We also learn socialization skills, how to get along with the other children, how to do what the teacher says, how to move from one project to another in orderly ways. At the beginning of our schooling, we step into a very large unknown world where everything is new and there is so much to be learned.

By the end of first grade, we've learned just the basics of reading, writing, and arithmetic. We're not yet proficient in any of these areas, nor are we expected to do more than the first grade level. We are not expected to know geometry, be able to write short stories, or diagram a sentence. Those expectations would be ridiculous because we're simply not yet capable of that level of learning.

Then we move into second grade and begin the year by reviewing what we already learned in first grade. We start slowly with some of the same skills we learned and then begin enlarging on those skills and adding mastery. Even so, while at the end of second grade we're much further along than in first grade, we're still not at the level of learning of a sixth grader. That's not expected of us. We learn only so much each year, and we begin the next year by reviewing what we've learned and then moving into new territory.

The way we move through the grades at school is a hologram for our soul's journey. We're not meant to learn all aspects of our soul lessons in one single lifetime. That's as ridiculous as saying we're supposed to master all of our schooling in one year. It just doesn't happen that way, nor is it meant to.

In school, we learn what is age-appropriate and grade-appropriate, and then we advance to the next grade and learn more. Likewise, we grow in each life, even those in which we seem to backslide or waste our time. Each life, regardless of how we live it, is a learning experience. Each life presents us with different facets of the lessons we're learning for our soul's development. We are challenged to grow through our greatest fears, which takes lifetimes.

This is how it is for us in "Earth School." As spiritual beings, we leave the spirit world and incarnate into a human body to learn and grow. The spirit world, heaven, is a place of unconditional love, peace, joy, and learning. The learning we do there is more theoretical than practical or experiential because no negative emotions, such as fear, greed, or resentment, get in our way. No obstacles or conflicts waylay us from our path of being Love. We learn the "theory" of how to handle situations in more loving ways, but we must be on earth to actually do the work itself, to remember to be Love and peace in the face of fear and loss.

It's true that some children excel in school, skip grades or move quickly into advanced studies. At the same time, other children hold back, repeating a grade because they're not ready for the more advanced work. They feel overwhelmed by school, or are simply not doing their homework.

In the same way, as souls, we may try to "skip ahead" and take on advanced lessons that can end up making our life extremely difficult. Or, we may do a "rest life" in which we're laid back and don't achieve much. I'll go into detail about this later in the book. All people are on their own spiritual path, following their soul's calling, learning what they need to learn here in earth school.

One of the great misunderstandings of reincarnation is that if you're having problems this lifetime, then it must be punishment for a life when you were bad. This is a misuse of the doctrine of karma – that is, the law of cause and effect. There is no punishment. Rather, reincarnation is a learning cycle that you have chosen. This truth can be very hard to swallow, especially when your life is filled with tragedies or heartaches. I want to introduce this important concept here:

Karma is learning, not punishment.

I have found from my clients that we all desire to learn and evolve as souls. The way we learn is most often through adversity and challenge, through risk-taking and stretching beyond what is comfortable or feels safe for us. Yes, we definitely grow through love and creativity, but most often, our soul grows the most by moving through fear.

This concept can be very upsetting. For example, what if a family has suffered a tragedy, such as the loss of a child? How can such a terrible event have been chosen? This is where the past life and life-between-lives viewpoints are so useful. They give us the "soul's long view," which means seeing the child's death in its much larger, many lifetimes' context.

From our human viewpoint, this death is tragic and heart-breaking. Absolutely! Yet, from the spiritual viewpoint, profound soul learning is possible. Often a death can spur a loved one onto their spiritual path. Perhaps, on the soul level, some members of the family came to earth school to learn to move beyond loss into being valuable contributors to their family or society. Or perhaps someone needs to forgive or to live alone or to accept help. Whatever the soul lessons for all the people involved, the event can make sense in the larger spiritual context.

We live in a dualistic Universe where we need to hold two truths at the same time. As humans we suffer pain and loss. On the other hand, as immortal souls, we desire to evolve ourselves, and that often requires that we experience pain and loss. Loss truly is bittersweet: We experience the physical pain as well as the spiritual fullness of growth. The more we are able to see both sides of ourselves – physical and spiritual – the more we can live life from a higher perspective, and the easier riding the waves of life's ups and downs becomes. I devote a later chapter to this very important subject, Our Balancing Act.

Believe it or not, feeling frustrated, stuck, and miserable may very well be the motivation you have needed to discover your life's purpose. You may even realize that if you can crack this puzzle, and learn the lessons you've come to learn in this life, you won't have to come back again and live yet another lifetime to learn these same lessons. You may say to yourself, "No matter what it takes, just let me know what I'm here to do so that I can do it NOW, because I'm not doing this again!"

Likely you will be back again – to learn other lessons. But for this lifetime, you are here for an important purpose. I hope you discover it reading this book.

2

Your Soul's Journey Between Lives

Your Soul has a calling, a purpose, which is fulfilling.

*Y*ou do not *have* a soul. You *are* your soul. Your soul is you, and it's more than your personality and your body. Part of your soul is inside your body, and a much, much larger part is outside your body. Your soul is consciousness, energy, light, part of the essence of God/Source/Infinite. Your soul is all that you have ever been. Some call it your Higher Self, others call it your spirit; you may call it by other names. You are not separate from your soul. Rather, you are contained within it.

There are various definitions for soul and spirit and the differences between them. Bob Olson, a friend of mine and author of *Answers About the Afterlife: A Private Investigator's 15-Year Research Unlocks the Mysteries of Life After Death*, has interviewed hundreds of psychics, mediums, people who have had near-death experiences, and others who have connections to the afterlife in one form or another. His book is based on the many interviews he has conducted, and in it, he answers 150 questions about the afterlife. As he notes in his book, the question that has received the most comments and interest is the difference between soul and spirit. Here is a small portion of his explanation:

"The soul is our whole self, the eternal and spiritual aspect of who we are.

The spirit is connected to each individual life's personality. It changes from lifetime to lifetime as we embody different personalities and bodies.

Each spirit has its own individual characteristics, but each will also have some common characteristics of its soul. Because of this, another soul will always be able to recognize a spirit's soul identity because of those signature characteristics.

Now taking this a step further, when I die, my spirit as Bob will leave my physical body and return home to the spirit world. In essence, my spirit will rejoin my soul and remain as an eternal aspect of my soul. In the same way that my human personality as a teenager is always present within me as an adult, my spirit as Bob will always be present in my soul."

So your soul is the wholeness of all that you are, encompassing the learning and growth and qualities you have developed throughout all your many lifetimes. Each lifetime, your soul creates a new spirit of itself to inhabit the new body. So your spirit is fully part of your soul, but your soul encompasses much more than who you are as this lifetime's spirit.

There is an ever-increasing interest in soul work. Do you believe it is your spirit or your soul that causes you to ask, "Just what is my life all about? Why am I here? Who am I really? Does my life make any sense? I know I'm here for something bigger, but what is that 'something'?"

Throughout this book I give examples from my clients who have asked this question, and received answers while in past life regressions or in the spirit world during a life-between-lives spiritual regression. We can learn from others' experiences because we are all in this together. We have all chosen to incarnate at this time and so we all have some things in common. The answers to "why am I here?" will differ among us, and at the same time, it's fairly universal that we all want to grow and develop in consciousness. We want to create and stretch ourselves in various ways. For some, this will be a more conscious choice to develop spiritually.

For others, spiritual growth will be unconscious because they aren't yet aware of being more than just their body. They think that what they experience with their five senses – what they see, smell, touch, hear, and taste – is all there is to life. They are not aware of cause and effect, and they don't yet know that their thoughts create their perceptions and thereby their life experiences. All this really doesn't matter in the big picture because, at some point in their spiritual development, they will learn. It may be this lifetime, or it may be another lifetime. In spirit, each life is but the blink of an eye.

As I cite client examples, notice how you are similar to them. Their life may not look like your life, but the same qualities exist within you as within them. We all have all of the qualities and characteristics known to mankind. Repeat:

We all have every characteristic, but it can show up differently in you than in others.

For example, you may be highly critical of critical people, and not even recognize how you criticize. Or you may think someone is a bully, and declare that you have never bullied anyone. But look at how you react to the bully and see if it is a kind of bullying.

Or perhaps you are a bully to yourself, constantly putting yourself down. My invitation is to look at yourself more closely as you read through this book, and try to find every quality mentioned in yourself, in whatever form you choose to express it.

You Pre-Planned This Life

You made plans before coming into this lifetime. Did you realize that? Your soul met with other wise and loving spiritual beings and helped you decide what you wanted to learn this time around. You may have gotten together with your guide(s) – spiritual beings who continually live in the spirit world – to discuss how you did last lifetime with your lessons and the next step for you to take in this lifetime.

It's likely you also met with your soul family – the group of loving beings that you "hang out with" in the spirit world. They know you, love you, and often incarnate with you. You all have discussions about the roles you want to play in each other's lives if you plan to incarnate together.

You also met with your elders – the group of very wise and loving beings who have known you throughout all of your lives. They know the much bigger picture of who you are as a soul and what you are trying to learn next. They advised and guided you on lessons, challenges, and opportunities you may face in this life.

With all this pre-planning you did, keep in mind one very important item: Free will. Yes, you as a soul have the free will to decide to come into another body or not. Your choice can be very difficult to face right now if you are having a challenging life. How many times have you wondered, "Whose idea was this?"

The answer: It was your idea. In the spirit world, it seemed like a great idea to take on all these challenges so that you could learn. It wasn't so that you would feel tortured or lead a miserable life. It was so that you could grow and develop as a soul.

I'll talk much more about choosing a challenging life in a later chapter on "fast trackers" – that is, souls who want to accomplish many lifetimes' worth of lessons in a single lifetime. I've worked with a number of people who fall into this category.

I used to explain this pre-life planning by saying: "Prior to coming into this lifetime, there was a big checkerboard in the sky that listed various lessons. We would check off what we wanted to learn in this lifetime." It wasn't anything I had read; it was simply an illustration I used. Imagine my surprise and delight when I saw it elsewhere.

I read Robert Schwartz's book, *Your Soul's Plan: Discovering the Real Meaning of the Life You Planned Before You Were Born*, in which he used very capable psychics and mediums to tune into the pre-planning activities of people with challenging lives. In one instance, he describes how a baby was accidentally blinded at birth, which was neither anticipated nor planned. (Yes, surprises happen!)

As Schwartz describes, the baby's spirit and his two guides then quickly had to re-plan his life. They used three large "chessboards" for planning his life: a lower one for the life that had been planned, listing all the planned steps of his growth and development; a middle transitional board where they moved possible scenarios from the planned life that would still fit his blinded life; and a top final board with the finished plan.

As Schwartz describes: "The boards are like a hologram – filmy in appearance, not solid. Their thoughts create these boards and draw lines on them. Lines represent the process of growth."

It's one of the most extraordinary descriptions of life planning I have ever read, and the description of the planning boards felt very familiar to me. I highly recommend his book, as it's fascinating reading.

Why would anyone plan for tragedies, heartache, loss, loneliness, addiction, betrayal, or any other sort of dismal life struggle? How can this all be planned, and why would we do that to ourselves? That's the real question, isn't it?

To be at peace with the thought that you planned a difficult life, you need to know that spiritual laws do not match physical laws. They are very different. On the physical level, it might look as though we are harming ourselves. On the spiritual plane, however, it's not seen as harm but rather as growth. When we move through challenges, we learn and grow. Plus, we gain a sense of satisfaction and achievement as we grow.

There is no intention of harm because on the spiritual plane, there is only Love. It is all Love. There is no death because the soul lives on. We are eternal in nature and upon returning to the spirit world after the end of a life, we return to Love. And yet, on the physical level, we can encounter great physical, psychological, and emotional harm done to one another. There are unconscionable acts of brutality in the news every day. This is true on the physical plane. Yet, at the very same time, in spirit, there is still only Love.

This is the duality people live with daily. It can cause concern, anger, confusion, helplessness, and even despair. How can we possibly perceive love and pre-planning in the midst of tragedy, terrorism, and brutality? If we do deep inner work, becoming willing to shift our perceptions and see the bigger picture of our lives by moving out of "right and wrong" thinking, then we can find the blessings and the balance in anything and everything that happens in our lives. This will make more sense as you continue through this book.

This "balancing of opposites" may challenge you deeply. If so, that's good, because you can have some deep insights and shifts in your life. If you are willing to let go of how you think your life should have been, you start to notice the gifts and design inherent in how it has unfolded.

I certainly don't have all the answers. What I do have, however, is many years of experience in leading clients into the super-conscious state of mind where they receive profound insights into their lives and the meanings underlying all they have experienced.

Experiencing a Life-Between-Lives Session

In 2000, I experienced a life-between-lives spiritual regression with Dr. Michael Newton, author of *Journey of Souls*. When I read his book two years earlier, I knew two things for sure: (1) I was born to do this work, and (2) I already knew how to do it; I just needed a session to "remember."

Since my own session, I have been doing this amazing work. I use hypnosis to guide people into a deep trance that enables them to access the super-conscious state of mind, which is beyond their subconscious knowing. In this deep trance, people clearly and vividly experience being in the spirit world, the "place" they go in between lives. I use the term "place" loosely because it's not a place; there is no specific location defined by latitude and longitude. Rather, it's accessed through a state of consciousness and is in "no place" and "no time."

I enable clients to remember their journey into the afterlife. I lead them back into a past life, through a few scenes in that life, and then through that death. In going through the death of that prior life, the client immediately feels a sense of relief, freedom, no longer trapped, lightness, expansion, or floating. It's an immediate release of the heaviness of being in their body.

At that point, in their life-between-lives journey, the client releases the body fully and begins the journey "home" to the spirit world. It really does feel like going home. It's a place we all know so well. We tend to forget it when we are in a body. But in the session, returning home can bring a tremendous sense of relief and joy when we are again united with our loved ones, spiritual teachers, and guides.

As you enter into the spirit world, deep healing occurs as you release the energies and emotions of having been in a physical body. Typically, there are beings of light that infuse or shower you with healing energy. Clients report that it feels warm, expansive, energizing, and absolutely loving. With this healing, you lose all feeling of being in a physical body and, once again, return to your spiritual state of being. You return to your fuller soul essence. It's as though you come home to yourself and suddenly feel whole and complete.

Typically, you spend time with your spiritual guide, a wise being who has known you for many lifetimes, reviewing the life you just lived. There is only Love; there is no judgment. These wise beings have deep understanding and compassion for your physical life experiences. That doesn't mean, however, that you aren't held accountable for your actions. There is definite accountability and consequences for the life just lived – but it's without judgment. You'll read more about this in the clients' experiences that follow.

You view your life from your soul's perspective:

- What you wanted to learn and how you did.
- How you treated others and the consequences of your actions.
- If you were stopped by fear, you have the opportunity to see options that you could not see during your life.

It's an objective and loving review of your life so that you can determine what you want to learn next.

When you're in the physical body, your attention can get consumed with pain, suffering, or fear. At the same time, you are trying to change your actions, be creative, follow your intuition, and create the fulfilling life you've dreamed about. In the spirit world, you are filled with compassion for the life you just lived, rather than judging yourself (as we tend to do when in a body).

One of the main reasons clients come to me for the life-between-lives spiritual regression is to learn their life purpose in their current lifetime. "What is my life all about?" is their primary question. They want to make sense of their life and be sure they are on target for the lessons and plans they made for this life.

In the spirit world, you meet with your council of elders, a group of extraordinarily wise beings who really know you. Some have been with you for eons, many lifetimes, or since the beginning of your journey. It's hard to know "how long" because time doesn't exist in spirit. The elders have been counseling you throughout many lifetimes and can see the bigger picture of your soul's journey. They are typically seen as figures of light and often have a sense of humor, while at the same time, understanding the trials of being in a human body.

They are the ones who typically help you remember and understand your life lessons and purpose for your current lifetime. They help you create order out of apparent chaos or "wrong doing" in this life.

I worked with a woman in her thirties whose beloved fiancé died a few years ago. She started off her questions to the elders with, "why was he taken from me?" She showed great courage as they slowly took her through her pain of loss and indignation that this had happened *to* her.

They were very clear, however: "He was not taken *from* you." It took a while for her life plan to unfold, but then she was very clear. "Oh, I chose this." She had known they would not be together very long. She not only chose to be with him, she "insisted" they be together, even though it would only be a short time.

She gained a deep understanding and clarity of the bigger picture and was able to recognize and fully own her plans and her insistence. Ah, yes, he was not taken from her. Their separation had been planned for the growth of both of their souls' journeys. After the regression, it was several months before she felt she could finally release him, but she did it in her own time and now feels very much at peace with it.

Deep peace comes with this sort of understanding and remembering. Healing also comes as a result of ownership, acknowledging that you set this plan in motion with full awareness of the outcome.

True, the planning was in the spirit world, where and when you were not feeling any sort of loss or pain.

As Above, So Below

I think that planning a life in the soul state is very much like setting any major goal here on earth. You think, "What a fabulous idea it would be to start this business!" You get excited as you see the potential, and you recognize the good that you can create for others. But then it gets difficult as you encounter the actual conditions of creating the business, or project, or whatever you are planning. Things don't go as planned. Unexpected crises occur. Fears overwhelm you and invade your life daily.

"This is no fun! Whose idea was this, anyway? I don't want to do this anymore. It is a dumb idea." Isn't this what we think as we encounter obstacles that keep us from what we desire to create?

The only way to turn your vision into reality is to push through your fears and setbacks. You automatically do this all the time – even if you haven't noticed. You learned to walk, ride a bike, read, write, and do math. You have pushed through barriers and obstacles your entire life because that's how life is. That's how we all learn: We move through the limitations of our old way of thinking and create from a new consciousness.

With any goal setting or creative process, it certainly helps to know what you want to create, so that you head in the right direction. It's the same with your life purpose. If you have a clear understanding of why you came into this body, you can make decisions that more clearly sync up with your life plans.

When I take clients into the spirit world, they heal and release emotional burdens because they realize what they set themselves up for in this lifetime. They often end up laughing – through the tears – and wondering, "What was I thinking?" From the human perspective, they planned a difficult and challenging life. Yet, as a soul, they were excited about the prospects of what they could gain in this lifetime.

Insights, knowledge, and wisdom I learned from my clients' experiences into the spirit world, as well as my own journey and years of study, are the basis for this book. My goal and intention are to help you see the bigger picture of who you are and the journey you are on in this lifetime.

Opening our hearts and minds to new information is what helps us grow in deeper and more meaningful ways. I hope and pray you find your lessons and purpose in life and come to a deep sense of peace and well-being that you are, indeed, on your soul's path. Let's get going as we delve into the vital roles that meaning and purpose have in your life.

3

Meaning and Purpose

"Everyone has his own specific vocation or mission in life to carry out a concrete assignment which demands fulfillment. Therein he cannot be replaced, nor can his life be repeated. Thus, everyone's task is as unique as is his specific opportunity to implement it." – Viktor Frankl

*Y*our life has meaning and purpose. This is true for each and every person alive, for those who have ever lived, and for those yet to be born.

You did not just willy-nilly decide to come into a body and endure decades of life on earth, regardless of how your life may seem at times. Clients' experiences in the spirit world confirm that you actually chose your family, your body, and your surroundings. You came into your body to learn and grow, to create and be inspired, and to be of service and care for others.

The dilemma for so many people, however, is:

WHAT am I meant to do?

This is the number one question I get from people who come to me for past life and life-between-lives sessions.

There is another group who come to me and already know what they want to do with their life. But, they can't seem to move forward and actually do it, for various reasons. So their question is:

HOW do I do what I'm meant to do?

You are probably familiar with the famous quote from William Shakespeare's *Romeo and Juliet*, in which Juliet says,

"That which we call a rose, by any other name would smell as sweet."

A rose is what it is; its job is to be a rose, no matter what you call it. Likewise, you are who you are. You have come into this life to be yourself, not someone else. You are not here to fulfill the hopes and desires of anyone else. Quite simply, you are here to be the rose that you are.

Some people are very driven to find and fulfill their life purpose. It's a source of deep pain and frustration to feel as though they are not accomplishing what they have come to be and do. I've worked with numerous clients who believed they "wasted" a past life and have therefore come into this life determined to not make that mistake again. In a past life they held themselves back in various ways:

- They were afraid.
- They ignored their dreams and did not live them.
- They listened to and/or obeyed what others wanted them to be or do.
- They isolated themselves physically or emotionally from the world.
- They held back from love and success.
- They lost themselves to alcohol or drugs and just waited around to die.

In their life-between-lives session with me, as they release their body at the time of death, each of these clients says the same thing as they look back at that life: "What a waste!"

However, as they move into the spirit world during our session, they learn from the spiritual guides they meet that no life is ever wasted because we all learn from our mistakes. These clients then realize that they actually benefited from their "wasted" life: They come into future lives with a desire to move through all obstacles and not let anything stop them. There is a strong underlying knowing that they don't want to again be disappointed in themselves at the end of their current life. So they are driven to fulfill their dreams and goals.

Many clients who have felt they wasted opportunities in a past life receive the following guidance from their elders in the spirit world:

*When your heart is open, your life will have
meaning no matter the circumstances.*

Does it feel daunting to think that your life has a life purpose – a single life purpose? If so, do you think your purpose has to be big, significant, impact large numbers of people, and change the world?

Well, I have good news. There isn't just one life purpose. You may have different purposes as you move through stages or phases of your life. Or, perhaps you have one overarching purpose with numerous lessons connected to it. Your purpose doesn't have to be big and significant. You will influence others (maybe many others), no matter what you do – if you follow your heart and soul. It can't be otherwise.

What Do You Value?

Your purpose in life coincides with what you value most. They go hand-in-hand. Have you thought about what you most value in life? The easiest way to know what you value is to look at three aspects of your life:

1. Your calendar
2. Your checkbook
3. Your surroundings

What you spend your time and money on, and what you surround yourself with, are what you most value.

For example, perhaps you think you value your family, but you actually spend little quality time with them. Rather, you spend all your time engrossed in work you love. This simply means you put more value into your work than your family. Or perhaps you value your paycheck and your financial security, rather than your work. You highly value providing for your family, and secondly, you spend your free time in sports or a hobby.

Or perhaps you work in a congenial workplace and find it more supportive than your family. So you prefer to spend time with your colleagues rather than go home at the end of the day. You value their friendship more than the environment you have at home.

In your logical mind, you may say you value one thing. But if you don't spend time or money on it, then perhaps you don't really value it. If that's the case, then look at your life to see what you actually do value.

Such honest thinking about what you truly value may cause you to feel guilty about your choices. But don't go down that path. Our culture professes high esteem for "family values," but is that just rhetoric? Do people espouse that value but actually live by another? Family may or may not be your number one value.

Here's the truth: There is no "best" value;
it doesn't work that way at all.

We are all on this earth to pay attention to our inner urgings and desires about what we enjoy and what brings us great satisfaction and a sense of well-being or achievement.

Here's a little exercise to hone in on your top few values:

- Take some time to look through your checkbook and your calendar for the past month. Where have you spent the most money and how have you spent your time?
- What do you do in your leisure time? You will gravitate toward what you most value.
- Look around your living space, or personal space within your home (such as your favorite chair, or bedside table). What do you surround yourself with? Do you have books on a certain subject, or on many subjects? Or perhaps you have a tablet that's filled with e-books that you read every chance you get. Do you have hobby supplies, or musical instruments, or technology gadgets strewn all over?

Your answers in these three areas demonstrate what you value.

And here's why knowing your top values is important: You make decisions based on what you most value, whether you are conscious of it or not.

Here's my current example as I write about values. My driveway is badly in need of repair. But I place very little value on resurfacing it. For months, I have put off calling anyone for a quote to do this work. And yet, in the space of *one hour*, I made a decision to fly to another state to attend a weekend personal development workshop. Why choose one and not the other? Spiritual transformation is my top value, so this travel decision was easy. In fact, the trip's cost is not a "show stopper" for me because I know I always find the resources to do whatever I most highly value. Meanwhile, the driveway remains unfixed.

Once you know your top three or four values, you will find it so much easier to make decisions. You just ask yourself, "Is this in line with my highest values?" This little test not only makes you more confident in your decisions, but you can also save yourself from making an unwise decision about something of low value for you.

Think back to your wedding and all the preparations for that big day. What was it you actually valued about that day? If you placed the highest value on making sure every little detail was perfect, why was that important for you? Did you value looking good? Perfection? Or was setting a high standard important to you? Really think about what was most important to you about your wedding and all the time and money you spent leading up to it. You may surprise yourself looking back on it.

Typically, it's the women who get wrapped up in the minutiae; although, some men absolutely get involved in the planning. Often, however, it's the bride urging and coaxing her groom to be interested in something he doesn't really care about. And then she can get her feelings hurt or feel unheard or unloved. He may value making sure his bride is happy, but the actual details are way down his list of values. If you know what holds high value for both of you – details high up in value for the bride, low in value for the groom – then you can have a different (probably far more productive) conversation about all the details.

You can tell the truth about what has value and meaning for you and what doesn't. Sometimes we need to step up and show up for those we love because it matters to them. So, for the groom, respecting and supporting what his bride values can be an act of love, which is what he highly values. Even though I use bride and groom as examples, this holds equally true for same sex couples. One can be interested and the other not. It's not about the gender of the person, it's about what each person values and doesn't value.

Your meaning and purpose in life are connected to what you most value. Values change over time. Just as the wedding preparations can be a top value for a year, taking up an extraordinary amount of time and money, when the big day is over, new values may arise. But the reasons why you valued the preparations may actually go far deeper than the wedding, and those values then show up in a different way in your life. That's why it's important to dig deeper and discover what you actually value.

I value the work of Dr. John Demartini on this subject and who he is as a person. Dr. Demartini is an author, educator, business consultant, leadership expert, specialist in human behavior, and founder of the Demartini Institute. You can go to his website *www.drdemartini.com* and take a free "value determination" quiz to help you see just what you value. It's very helpful to get clear on what you actually value, not just what you think you should value but don't. He has written numerous books that include his values work, most especially, *The Values Factor: The Secret to Creating an Inspired and Fulfilling Life.*

I have discovered that the time I have spent reading his books and attending his trainings have been both life-affirming and soul-affirming because he has helped me ferret out my highest values, which has made me much clearer on my purpose and meaning in this lifetime.

What Matters Most

We are all energy beings, emanating energy outward all around us. When you are involved in your passion and following your heart, you emit a high level of energy. You can't help but influence others, even though you may not realize it. When your heart is open, when you are doing what you love and value, then you will find meaning in everyday life.

Let's say you love to make jewelry. Years ago, I conducted a life-between-lives session with a woman who was passionate about bringing beauty into the world. But she thought that making jewelry wasn't a "big" enough life purpose.

During her session, her spirit guides explained to her that bringing beauty into the world was her purpose, her joy, and her gift to those who bought her creations. In being creative, she inspired others to be creative. She was being of service to all who enjoyed wearing her jewelry, and, on some level, to those who were aware of the energy of love and creativity she put into each piece she made. When she heard this, she realized that what she loved to do, what she lived for, was actually "important enough" to be her life purpose – and she visibly relaxed and became peaceful in our session.

Caroline Myss, author of many spiritual writings and a gifted mystical teacher, talks about how people want an *important* life purpose. As a result, they can miss what is right in front of them to do. In one of her talks, she said, "What if you are to be a bright light in your neighborhood?"

That statement made a big impression on me. Not long after I heard her say that, I was at a weekend workshop and was talking with a woman who was searching for her life purpose. She talked about how her home was the one that all the neighborhood children came to, and, at times, it felt like a madhouse. She didn't want all her time taken up with mothering the neighborhood children. She wanted to get on with her life purpose, to do something *important*.

So I talked to her about what Caroline Myss had said about being a bright light. I told her that so many of my clients could remember looking back to one adult in their childhood who had been their saving grace, providing them a refuge from their difficult families. I told her that she couldn't possibly know the incredible influence she was having on each of her neighborhood children.

As we walked and talked, she could see that she was their bright light, and that just what she was doing naturally was obviously her life purpose at that time. Later, when the children were no longer coming to her home, then she would be led to "what's next." But in the meantime, she was right on target with doing what was most important. It can be that simple.

Examples of Life Purpose

Following are examples of life purpose gleaned from over a thousand spiritual regressions I have conducted over the past 15 years. What I find striking about them is how simple and straightforward they are. And yet, they can take lifetimes to achieve. In addition, notice that none of them is related to jobs or careers.

- Be yourself, even in difficult times and circumstances
- Listen to your heart, follow your heart's desires
- Realize your mind, body, spirit connection
- Keep the connection to the spirit world open, always know it's there
- Live from compassion, regardless of circumstances or human behavior
- Keep one's heart open and hold deep love in the midst of being broken-hearted or hurt
- Let go and trust
- Love yourself
- Trust yourself, believe in yourself, have faith and confidence in yourself, know your self-worth
- Have a sense of yourself
- Trust others (often learned through betrayal)
- Trust the Universe
- Move through fear
- Find happiness and meaning in spite of being alone and lonely
- Connection: to self, others, and spirit
- Quieting the mind; "being" rather than "doing"
- Recovering from devastation; rebuilding after shattering
- Rest, self care
- Take life less seriously, less intensely – have more fun
- Set healthy boundaries, for self and others

- Listen, pay attention, to feelings and inner guidance
- Listen, pay attention, to others (rather than being narcissistic)
- Stop hiding or holding yourself back
- Create
- Find balance
- Be well, naturally
- Acceptance (often of life, on life's terms)
- Release struggle, suffering, sacrifice
- Experience joy, delight, happiness

These are not complex or difficult to comprehend, are they? Each is quite simple in nature, but certainly not easy to master. Together, they illustrate the aspects we require to live from a state of Love rather than fear. As people master the qualities and characteristics that form their own life purpose, they embody Love more fully in all its forms and in all situations. Each lifetime is spent working toward one or more specific embodiments of Love, as listed above. You are definitely not meant to learn all forms of Love in one lifetime. Sometimes, just one Love-based purpose is plenty.

As you went through the list, did one or more of these purposes give you a chill, or strike a chord in you? If so, pay attention. Can you quickly think up at least five events or situations in your life that have had the express purpose of teaching you that life purpose? If you get quiet inside, ask yourself to see how your life has set you up with countless opportunities to learn what you have come to learn – and perhaps master.

You Make It All Up

As you look through that list, you get to decide what rings true for you. Here's what is actually true about your life purpose: You make it up. Yes, you decide what your life purpose is. Let me repeat: *You get to make it up*. It may feel true and you may know it to the depth of your soul, but you're still making it up. And that's OK. We make everything up.

Life is neutral, events are neutral, and situations are neutral. We individually put meaning into our lives, the events, and the situations we find ourselves in.

Do you really understand what that means for you? You are making it all up – so make it up good!

Your beliefs and perceptions – you made them up. You gave meaning to what people told you as a child and to what you experienced in any moment in time. The look your mother gave you – you made it mean something about you. The way you father acted at the dinner table – you made it mean something about you. The way your siblings teased you – you made that mean something about you, too. You've made up all your perceptions, and in just the same way, you make up your life purpose.

This is great news: You get to decide what to do with your life! There isn't something or someone "out there" who is determining your future or deciding if you do well or not. There is just you, all of you, including your soul/higher self, on this path of life.

Yes, you may feel a definite urge to go in a certain direction. So do that.

You may have no idea what you are meant to do. If so, then ask yourself:

What would I LOVE to do?

And stop thinking it has to be some grandiose plan. Your purpose can be very simple. It can even be just a way of being, rather than doing something.

Years ago, I led a session with a woman, Carol, who came to me for a spiritual regression because she wasn't sure what job she should do to fulfill her life purpose. So many people have the notion that their work job has to be their life purpose. Yes, for some, their work is a big part of their life purpose. But for many, it's not about a job but rather about developing qualities and characteristics for how to "be."

Carol was very surprised to find that her life purpose is to be "a loving presence," to be a beacon of love. It's something she does naturally. She understood that it didn't matter what job she took because she could be a loving presence in any setting, doing any type of work. She just needed to find work that she enjoys, and know that it's secondary to what she's actually there to do. This knowledge gave her a great sense of peace and ease. She no longer had to worry, "Am I on my path?"

I have worked with many people in the healing arts, from chiropractors, to physicians, energy workers, psychics, transformational coaches, and healers. Because healing comes so naturally to them, they often want to make it their life work, and think it's their purpose. It may be part of their purpose, but there is always more to life than one's work.

People often think there is just *one* purpose they have come for, and if they don't find it and do it, then they have failed at this life. This is not true in many ways.

I will say this again:

> *You make up what things mean,*
> *and you make up how they matter.*

There is no one inherent meaning of anything that is true for everyone. So make it up good!

Finding Meaning

I think most of us go through phases in our life when it all seems meaningless. We have a sense of "what's the use?" I went through this for several years in my early fifties. My main thinking was: "What does it matter? In the end, we just die. So nothing really matters." I was going through the motions of living. But when I was alone, I thought that nothing I was doing really mattered. Part of my thinking was true: In the end, we do die. But what matters most is what we are doing before we die. How we choose to live.

How do you move out of such pervading negative thoughts and the accompanying depression?

What I did was pray for help. I believed that (1) my thinking was never going to make me happy or feel fulfilled in life, and (2) I didn't know how to combat my beliefs. They felt like the truth at the time. So in praying for help, I asked to see life differently. I asked to feel deeply within me, "Life matters." I knew I needed spiritual intervention to help me again see the sacredness of life.

I had no grand *aha* moment of enlightenment. I don't even remember how it happened. But I did gain a new perception of life. I do remember that I looked at the small things in life, the everyday events and interactions with people, and I mentally talked to myself about how they all mattered. I was very conscious of my inner dialogues. I would make myself look for how things mattered to me.

I realized that things mattered because I told myself they mattered. As I thought it, I began to feel it inside. I could feel the sacredness of beauty, and I reminded myself that beauty was important. Beauty matters to us human beings. I became conscious of the impact I was making on the lives of my clients, and I knew that what I said and did mattered in their lives.

This is a spiritual process. You walk out of meaninglessness and into meaning when you decide to take the journey. For a while, it may need to be a daily, conscious act of looking for and deciding that things matter and why they have meaning for you. Then it becomes more a way of being. You can feel it in your heart as you look around, feeling gratitude and knowing that you matter in the world.

So many times we think we have to do or be more, or bigger, or more grandiose. We need to be changing the world, having thousands of people participating in our work, or having 100,000 social media followers. We think that only then we will be doing our life purpose and our life will have real meaning.

Actually, the Universe often works in paradoxes. The person with thousands of social media followers may not actually have the same quality effect as when you take the time to talk to one neighbor. You may change that neighbor's life by something you say. Your communication is meaningful and it can matter greatly to your neighbor. What gives life meaning is not so much about quantity, as about quality.

A More Advanced Approach

If you already believe that your life matters and has meaning, you may be ready to step into a more advanced level of creating meaning in your life. This is the practice of giving positive meaning to *every* thing that occurs in your life. This doesn't mean to "think positive" no matter what happens, because that's often denial and takes you off center. It's much deeper thinking. The mindset I'm talking about is that, regardless of what happens, know that it is part of your spiritual path and it is an opportunity for you to grow. The "worse" something appears to be on the human level, the "better" – or more growth-oriented – it may be for you as a soul.

How quickly and easily you rebound from life's challenges depends on the meanings and purposes you give the challenges. If you can see everything, and everyone, in your life as assisting in your growth in some way, then you will more quickly and easily turn challenges into triumphs, tragedy into gratitude, and failure into growth.

Think about living from the mindset:

"Everything that occurs in my life is for my benefit."

What would it be like to live in this sort of consciousness? I'm not talking about just intellectually knowing this principle that it's all for your highest good. I'm talking about living from this consciousness every day. When things go well, they are for your benefit and growth. When things do not go well, they are also for your benefit and growth.

Take, for example, the following circumstances or behaviors that initially appear to be negative and limiting. Notice the surprising benefits that result:

- If a child isn't allowed to speak up in childhood, she can become highly skilled at listening to others and hearing their underlying messages. She may also become very outspoken as a result of having had her voice squelched.
- If a boy is told he's stupid or a slow learner, he may work extra hard at improving his learning abilities and become an expert in his field.
- Rather than giving up, someone who has experienced obstacle after obstacle can acquire great resiliency and inner strength to get back up again and keep going no matter what occurs.
- Someone who is bullied or put down verbally may go on to become a staunch defender of the underdog or the less fortunate.
- A person who has battled with eating disorders can learn a deeper level of self-love.

In all of these situations, the people put high value on the benefits that came from overcoming their obstacles. They are grateful for who they have become as a result of what life brought to them.

Could you live from this mindset when life continually challenges you year after year after year, in all areas of your life? I'm not saying I could do it all of the time, but I do believe this principle is Truth: We are constantly guided and situations are set up to bring us into alignment with who and what we have come into this life to be and do.

Just because life throws us curve balls doesn't mean we are doing anything wrong. It could be that we are learning how to rebound again and again. Know this:

There is no failure in spirit;
there is only learning and growing.

We often learn by what we don't do correctly, so each circumstance or life situation can propel us forward. That's a way of looking at your life from a higher consciousness, rather than from the thought, "I'm not good enough."

You get to look at your life and give it meaning. Know that authentic meaning is never based on harm or undermining others. It is based on being of service and love to yourself and others. So if someone is taking from others, manipulating and controlling circumstances for their own benefit, their life's meaning is *not* to teach others to be *not* so gullible. Even if that is the outcome, I believe that our life purpose is never meant to harm others. That flies in the face of Love, which is the essence of the Universe.

The Lifelong Thread

I have spent many years helping people see the bigger picture of their life journey, looking at their life from their soul's perspective. I firmly believe, and it's been my experience with all the spiritual regressions, that we all come into this life with a clear knowing and desire for what we want to learn and accomplish. This knowing and purpose reside within us, even though we may not consciously remember.

Because this knowing is within us, we have been following the thread since childhood. I have recently begun doing a new type of hypnosis session where I take people back to the root cause of when they first realized their life purpose. We then follow the thread of that purpose through their life, as various memories come to their mind. It's an amazing process, deeply moving, and quite validating to relive the memories from the viewpoint of seeing the thread of one's life purpose. I see it help change clients' perspectives on why different events occurred. It's healing – and often a relief – to understand it was all part of the bigger picture.

As I was explaining the process to one client at the beginning of the session, the words "be well" jumped into her head. As she then went into hypnosis and back to the first time she knew her life purpose, she went to her point of birth.

A nurse was sticking something down her throat and she believed the nurse was trying to kill her. In that first moment of life, she became aware on a deep level that she wanted to live. She wanted to live! (Many years later, when reliving her birth in a hypnosis session, she realized that the nurse was actually saving her life, clearing out the gunk in her lungs.) But in the moment of birth, the threat of death brought her clarity that she wanted this life.

She then followed the thread of health through childhood memories of loving being alive, as well as getting allergy testing and allergy shots, which she did not love. She remembered how much she didn't want that medical intervention. As she aged, her memories moved to the miracle of giving birth to her daughter, and how deeply she wanted her child to be healthy.

When she later became introduced to alternative healing modalities, she saw the progression of her interest in natural healing remedies and solutions. She has now become an activist in the cause of having choice over vaccinations. She had resisted getting out into the world in such an active and controversial way. As a result of seeing this activity as part of her life purpose, though, much of her resistance and fear washed away.

She experienced a quick, deeply moving, and emotional journey through her life in this session. In re-experiencing these few events, she sobbed while explaining many of the scenes to me. Such sobbing is often one's soul expressing, "This is real, this is truth." She was amazed to see that the activities that came up naturally in her life had been "on purpose" ever since the moment of her birth.

I have seen how this short process of looking back over your life to find the threads that have led you to where you are today is actually astonishing. It can leave you in awe and in deep-seated gratitude for knowing that your life purpose has been unfolding and solidifying, as you have just "lived your life naturally." It's right there. You can find it.

Try this yourself:

1. Draw a horizontal line on a piece of paper. This is the timeline of your life.
2. Get quiet inside and have the intention to follow the thread of your life purpose.
3. Ask yourself: What am I here to be or do? What is my purpose?
4. Allow yourself to sit quietly with the question and do not seek out the answer. Rather, let the answer come to you. This is not a process of figuring it out; it is a process of allowing it to reveal itself. You may already be very aware of your purpose. But if you still question it because it doesn't seem big enough or it is not happening in the time frame or manner in which you want, put those concerns aside for the time being because they are limiting your thinking.
5. As you sit quietly, notice the first memory that comes to mind. Write down the age and just a few words about the memory.
6. Move to the next memory that pops into your head. Let each memory come from inside you, not from your logical

or analytical mind. Give yourself time to review your life. Don't force a memory because you think it should be there. Just keep moving from one memory to the next, starting in early childhood through your life to the present.

When you have completed your timeline, look at it for patterns of situations, interests, or behaviors (yours or others) that have meandered through your life. If something comes up again and again as an interest or passion, or even as a situation that occurs over and over again, know that there is a reason for this pattern.

For instance, if you look over your life and realize that you have moved and/or started over from scratch on numerous occasions throughout your life, realize that you are trying to learn something. There is purpose and meaning for you in starting over again and again and again.

Or, perhaps, you played schoolhouse as a child and were always the teacher. Look for the pattern of teaching others throughout your life, even if you are not a teacher by profession. You are still a "teacher" in other areas of your life. Honor that passion. Maybe it is calling you to do more teaching.

Your life purpose is not hidden; it is in plain sight, and has been since childhood. You have more than one lesson and one purpose in your life, so start with the most obvious one and let it sink in deeply. It is what your soul is calling you to pay attention to and take action on.

The value in knowing your life purpose is that you have an inner compass to help you steer your life in a direction that fulfills your soul's longing. When you are aware of your purpose, you can't help but feel the meaning in your life as you move through life being yourself. You will more naturally make choices based on your higher awareness of what will lead you to the greatest sense of completion. Plus, you will be of service to others in a more conscious and fulfilling manner.

You have this knowing of your purpose within you. Getting quiet inside, doing inner work to release your limiting thinking, listening to your heart and what you deeply desire, and being conscious of what makes you feel alive will lead you to a sense of fulfillment throughout your life, as well as at the end of your life. To feel fulfilled with your life, nothing is more important than having meaning and purpose. It's within your ability to uncover your soul's calling.

4

Guidance and Intuition

*"Everything in the universe is within you.
Ask all from yourself."* — *Rumi*

*H*ow does your soul speak to you? How do you know when it is your soul calling you to be or do something, or if it's your ego mind, or just your imagination?

Everyone has access to his or her inner wisdom. These answers don't come from our logical mind, though. We receive them in other ways. When we get an intuitive answer, we don't know how or why we know something to be true. We just know it. We can feel its truth deep within us.

Before we learn to trust our intuition, we tend to think the knowledge may not be legitimate. How can we trust information when we don't know its source? So we don't act on it. We don't trust our own knowing and we wait for proof. In fact, sometimes we demand proof before we will take action. Mistrusting ourselves is part of the process we go through in our journey to learn how to trust and act upon the soul guidance we receive.

We are evidence-based. We want to be able to point to a legitimate, logical, proven source of how and what we know. Then we will act. This is how we have been taught to survive in the world – be logical, be rational, use your brain.

In using your intuition – your gut knowing – you do not throw away your reasoning and analytical mind. You may use your logical mind to study the facts, make reasonable sense of a situation, and analyze the possible outcomes. But so many times, this isn't enough. You still don't know what to do. You can't reach a decision based on analysis alone. This is where your intuition and guidance step in. Your intuition provides you with information above and beyond what you know logically, and thereby affords you guidance that you cannot get any other way.

However, we pretend we don't know what we're supposed to do. Haven't you pretended you didn't know what to do, but you actually did know? You just didn't want to do it. We sometimes (often?) resist doing what we are guided to do.

Resistance is Futile

Resistance plays quite a role in my own life. How about you? Do you resist much that occurs in your life? Do you think that things are happening too quickly, and you want to slow it all down? Or perhaps the opposite is true for you. Opportunities are not coming quickly enough, or you have felt stuck and held back from following your life purpose.

I know resistance well. Even as I started to write about this subject, I got up and decided it was more important to clean the kitchen counter, which, by the way, was already clean. I'd gone to the White Mountains in New Hampshire for three days to write, staying at a friend's vacation condo. There was nothing for me to do there but write. The entire kitchen was already clean, so I wasn't actually doing anything constructive; although I must admit that the first day there I alphabetized the spices and put them in nice neat rows. On another occasion, as I was writing this book in my own home, I decided it was imperative that I clean the kitchen stove and rearrange the bathroom shelves.

This was resistance at work. I'm sure you have your own ways of resisting.

Resistance shows up in many ways in our lives. I resist doing what I know is best for me. I resist doing my own inner healing work when I know I'm stuck; although I willingly help others work through their issues. And I resist changes, even though I welcome them at the same time. I just like to decide what the changes will be, rather than having life surprise me with them.

What do you resist, both on a small scale (as in daily habits) and in the larger picture of your life (as in life purpose)? Do you resist letting go of what isn't working for you, even when you know better?

Anytime I resist, I already know what would be a better action. It's not that I don't know. It's not that you don't know. We do know. We do listen to our inner guidance. The trouble is: We don't follow it.

We also receive a higher level of guidance that I call "listening to spirit." It's not just our mind or our common sense. It's the spirit world talking to us.

My sister recently gave me a small example of listening to spirit – and acting on it. She was in a church class called Prosperity Plus, which has ten weeks of one-hour videos by Mary Morrissey. In the sixth week, Mary talked about her interpretation of the David and Goliath story in the Bible. Only a few hours after that class, my sister was trolling her Internet news feed when she saw the words "David and Goliath." The reference was to a book, which happened to be written by one of her favorite authors, Malcolm Gladwell. She immediately ordered it on-line and discovered that its stories were just what she needed to read, because she felt she was a David facing a Goliath in her life. She, like so many people, has a spiritual practice of saying, "Thank you, Spirit," affirming where guidance comes from.

I have spent much of my life learning to listen to spirit speaking within me. This has been a long journey. I believe I started listening to spirit when I was nine years old. I was in church and I knew, from somewhere deep within me, that the minister was not connected to God. For me, he was doing damage because of his lack of connection. And I became confused. Why did I know our minister's disconnection, but my mother and the other adults didn't? This paradox made no sense to me.

One Sunday, I fainted in church, had to be carried out, and from that time forward I got to spend church in the nursery with the little kids. Imagine that! My inner resistance to that minister had gotten me out of his presence. Some years later, he was fired from his position. Listening to spirit was important to me as a child, even before I understood it intellectually. It has remained important to me ever since.

What's the difference between listening to spirit, guidance, angels, God, our intuition, and our gut knowing? Here's my best answer to that question: I don't know. I don't always know where the guidance comes from, and I don't actually care. As long as it is based in love, rather than fear, and truth rather than ego, I don't have to know the exact source. (But in this chapter I will tell you what I do know about these various sources.)

For all of us, listening to your intuition or guidance comes in many forms. See which ones you have experienced:

- An idea just pops into your head.
- You feel a sensation in your body, perhaps in your stomach or "truth chills" run up and down your spine.
- Your attention is randomly drawn to an Internet post or an item on a shelf.
- You hear the same thing from three different sources in a short period of time.
- You know the answer to a question before it is asked or while it is being asked.
- You dream of a spiritual being talking to you.

- You buy something and do not know why, only to discover later it's the perfect thing for: dinner for a guest you would invite in two days, a present for a friend's birthday you had forgotten about, the needed ingredient in a recipe you later spotted in a magazine.
- You hear a tiny voice and you *know* it is spirit – no question about it.
- You immediately get a warm or cold feeling about something or someone.

When these sensations happen, pay attention. You are being directed to specific information, so it could be in your best interest to listen, notice, and then take appropriate action. Often times, these inner whisperings are a possible answer to an unresolved issue, confirmation of a decision to be made, comfort about an agony, or an action for you to take.

All my years of listening to my guidance and intuition in simple ways prepared me for some of the bigger callings I have received.

In 2011, I was fixing up the front landscaping of my house. It was the first time I had ever put money into landscaping and I was very pleased with the effect. As I stood and admired my front yard, that clear voice inside me said, "This will make it sell faster." Oh no! Instant vehement resistance! "I am NOT moving," I growled inside myself.

A few weeks later, as I added more flowers and enjoyed my front yard, the voice came again: "The new owners will love it." "No!" I thought. "I am not fixing up my house so someone else can enjoy it." But, I actually knew better because I knew what the voice of spirit sounded like.

Two months later, on New Year's morning, as I woke up my first thought was a clear voice inside me: "Sell the house."

When you have done enough internal spiritual work, you know the difference between your ego's voice and your soul's voice. There is a different quality in the message. With spirit, the thought is quiet, no emotion, short, and to the point. There's no story about what will happen or why it needs to occur. It's just a short declaration. And often it is just said once. "Sell the house."

I had been warned those few months earlier as I stood in my front yard, so I didn't resist this guidance. I made a declaration: I would go through this process as an exercise in my spiritual growth. I placed three conditions on myself:

1. I would say, "Yes" and do whatever I was led to do.
2. I would not allow fear to enter into the process.
3. At the end of selling my house, I would be very proud of how I did #1 and #2.

This is how life works when you put resistance aside and you step fully into what you are being led to do. I did not ask any questions about where I would move or how I would sell the house. I just started the process. Since I was doing this as a "game" of listening to spirit, I followed the "rules" as I understood them, as they unfolded within me. I knew I was not to look for another house yet. And I knew my house would sell in May. So I went on vacation across the country in May, and sure enough, that's when the offer came in. The sale was to close on June 18.

At this point, resistance could have played a role – but I chose differently. I knew I was being led by spirit, so I continued on my vacation for nine more days. I had no place to move; although, friends offered me shelter if I got caught without a home. It was nice to have a plan B, but I hoped I wouldn't need it. Plan A was to find a home and move in before my house closed.

When I returned home, I went looking at houses with my realtor and friend, Karen Lilly. We looked at a couple of places and then were invited to join other friends for margaritas and guacamole. That sounded like much more fun than house hunting.

The next day was Saturday and Karen was unavailable, so another friend and I had a great time looking at houses.

Sunday morning, I woke up and realized I knew *exactly* what I wanted. I wanted a house with an in-law apartment, so I would have rental income. I also knew the particular area I wanted to live in, and I knew the top price I would pay.

I sent my list off to Karen, and to the Universe, and she responded that night by email with the subject line: "Bingo!" She found one house that matched my description. We saw it the next morning, made an offer that evening, and it was accepted within a day.

Here is the kicker to this story: The wife was in the military and was being transferred to California. The family needed to rent their house until it sold, which was going to take several months because it was going through a special military short-sale program. They had to continue paying their mortgage, so I rented their house until the sale closed and I owned it. They moved out on Thursday, June 14. I moved in on Friday, June 15. My own house closed on Monday, June 18. That's how guidance and divine timing can work with ease and flow.

Through this experience, I affirmed that there are ways to go through life where we don't resist and are not afraid. And it's our choice. My house-moving experience was a powerful learning for me. It was all handled in divine timing. I didn't know all the details of what would unfold. But, by not resisting, by going along and saying, "Yes," each step unfolded in perfection.

When we resist and become fearful, we clog the flow. We get in our own way, and then wonder why things aren't working out well.

If you know you are being called to do something and you are filled with fear or indecision, why not make up some rules for yourself? Decide how you want to show up for the challenge and/or opportunity and how you want to feel at its completion. Rather than focus on what has been stopping you, act as though you are in charge of the "rules" of the game and how you will play it. Listen to your guidance and intuition and take actions based on your inner knowing. If you're unsure that your guidance is authentic, later in this chapter I'll talk about the differences between the voices of intuition and ego.

5 Yeses

I had one of the most extraordinary spiritual experiences of my life at the end of 2005. I suddenly found myself in front of my spiritual council of elders in the spirit world. It was extraordinary in that it takes me well over an hour of using hypnosis to get clients into this state of consciousness. Yet I was there in the blink of an eye. I remember thinking, "Is this real?" I knew it was. I had been there in my own life-between-lives session five years prior. So I knew what was happening; although it felt quite surreal to be there so unexpectedly.

My elders showed themselves to me as five very wise beings, extremely loving and also "businesslike" in their communications with me. They wanted me to know that I had completed the lessons I had originally intended for this lifetime. They telepathically let me know that they hadn't expected me to completely learn these lessons for another twenty years, when I would be in my mid-seventies. They asked, "Do you want to continue with this life or are you ready to come home to spirit?"

To this day I am still grateful that I had the presence of mind to ask a very simple question, "What did I do that accelerated my learning?" They showed me five simple, yet pivotal, decision points when I said "yes" to their guidance.

1. In late 1997, I hurt my toe and asked my body what it was trying to tell me. The very clear reply was, "You're not taking your steps." I ignored that advice.

    Six weeks later I broke that same toe, which was my first broken bone in my life. I again asked for the message from my body and received the same answer, which I again ignored.

Two months later, I was hurrying with my friends to get to a restaurant before losing our dinner reservations. The sidewalk was cracked and uneven, and in my rush, I fell headfirst and skidded my chin along the pavement. Time stopped. Clear as a bell, I heard a voice tell me, "Next time, it's a full body accident."

My immediate inner response was, "OK, you win, but I can't quit my job. I love those people too much. But if you take it from me, I won't fight it."

I knew I was to leave my job, but I still felt quite secure because I was performing at a high level. Two months later, my company re-organized and, to cut expenses, the new director decided to combine my job with another manager's job. I was offered the position, but declined it. Within weeks I was laid off. I said "yes" to leaving my work.

2. A few months later, I went camping by myself in Yellowstone National Park and the Grand Tetons. I spent two weeks in near silence, often spending an hour or two just waiting for a geyser to erupt for a few moments. Being in nature felt sacred, and I more clearly heard my inner voice.

On my drive home, I realized I had a choice: I could double back and go through the Grand Tetons and Jackson Hole again and then home to California through Utah and Nevada, or I could continue on westward through Idaho and Oregon as I had originally planned. As I was looking at the map, I again heard a very clear voice, "You have free choice, but your future lies through Idaho and Oregon. Going through Jackson Hole is off your path. It's your choice."

The minute I decided to continue westward, I started crying. Some deep part of me, my soul, knew it was an important decision. I said "yes" to my future.

3.   Two days later, I drove into Bend, Oregon, and knew I had to live there for a time. A month later, I packed my car as full as I could and moved to Bend, where I rented a tiny trailer for three months.

I spent most of my time in silence, in nature, journaling, drawing, and anything else I felt led to do. I said "yes" to moving away from my long-time home (California) temporarily.

4.   While living in Bend, I started seeing a hypnotherapist to help me through a number of my blocks because I was feeling quite stuck in life. I loved working with her. I felt changes happening in every session.

After I'd seen her for six weeks, she suggested that I take the hypnosis training myself. On a Wednesday, I looked it up online and found a month-long residential training starting that coming Saturday in northern California. I thought to myself, "There's not enough time to do that." And again, that clear voice said something like, "What else are you doing with your time?" So I called the training office, but it was after office hours, so I couldn't get more information.

On Thursday morning, I got up early, washed my clothes, and started packing my belongings. I made arrangements to leave some of my belongings in the storage shed in the trailer park. When I finally called about the hypnosis training, I gave them my credit card number because I had already decided to go before even talking with them.

When I hung up, I started sobbing. Again, something deep inside of me knew I had just changed the course of my life. The next day, I drove ten hours to the training, and Saturday morning I started on the next chapter of my life work. I said "yes" to the hypnosis training.

5.   Six months later, my husband and I knew our time together had ended and we decided to divorce. I pulled out a map of

the United States, along with my pendulum for dowsing, and said, "OK, God, you've got me. Where do you want me?"

I was confident that spirit would want me somewhere in the western United States. Boy was I *shocked* when the pendulum led me to Cape Cod on the east coast, as far from California as I could possibly move. All I could shout was, "NO! West Coast!!" For three days I asked, "Where do you want me?" and each time I clearly heard, "Cape Cod."

I kept resisting until I heard that clear voice inside me say, "My good waits for me in Cape Cod." With that clarity, I immediately changed my tune, and less than two months later, I was living in Cape Cod. I said "yes" to my good.

On their own, none of these five "yes" decisions was monumental. But within eighteen months, they stacked together to propel me forward along my path. At any point, I could have said "no," and I would still have been on my path of learning – just at a slower pace.

At the time of each decision, I had no way of knowing how much it would change my life. I had an inkling that something big was happening on a soul level, because I cried so deeply and unexpectedly. Those outbursts clued me in to realizing that I had just done something important for my growth. But that's all I knew. I received no details.

That's a big aspect of listening to our soul's calling: We don't know the outcome. When we don't know the results of a decision, we often resist saying "yes" *until* we feel comfortable that we can handle whatever perceived changes await us.

But waiting until we're comfortable, or have everything figured out, isn't usually how spirit works. We are called to step out into the unknown because that's how we best grow, create, and expand. We are *meant* to be uncomfortable and to feel afraid. That's part of the learning.

Creativity and expansion occur in the unknown. If you already know how to do everything you feel called to do, where is the growth and learning? Where is the creativity if you just do the same things you've always done?

The Voices of Guidance

You may read my story of hearing a clear voice and think, "I don't hear that voice inside me," or "I don't have that ability." Here's the Truth: We can all access our inner wisdom and the voice of our soul calling to us. I'm not special. There aren't just some of us who can listen to our guidance. We *all* have an inner voice.

Everyone *can* listen, but not everyone *does* listen. Our still small voice of spirit is part of being human. We are more than a physical being; we are a spiritual being who has poured our true self into this physical form for a time here on earth.

If there's one piece of advice and counsel that nearly every single client receives on their journey into the spirit world, it is this: Meditate more. Spend time each day being quiet, stilling your noisy thinking mind.

You can't hear your inner voice:

- When your mind is busy with thoughts of what you need to do;
- When you are thinking about what somebody said or did to you;
- When you are internally complaining about what's wrong with the country, or the government, or your neighbor;
- When you are worried about how you are going to pay your bills;
- When you are wondering, "What if something goes wrong with my plans?";
- And on and on and on, ad nauseum.

It's difficult to hear clearly when your mind is busy 24/7. Quiet your mind for five minutes a day. Everyone has time for that. This is not a news flash. This is not new information. Nearly everyone is told this by their council of elders. The ones who aren't told to meditate more are the ones who are already doing it – and listening as closely as they can.

If you're unsure how to meditate, or think you can't do it because of your noisy mind, then start very simply. Just follow your breath. That's it. As you breathe in, notice the sensation of the air entering in through your nose. Really feel your breath entering your body. Listen to it. How does your breath sound? Feel the expansion of your lungs as you breathe in fully.

Then follow your breath down and out of your body as you exhale. Repeat the process with your next breath, and the next, and the next. When you notice yourself thinking – and your mind will start to get busy – simply come back to observing your breath. As you're waking up or falling asleep, you can spend five minutes being conscious of your breath and quieting your mind.

You don't need to go off by yourself for two weeks or three months to hear your soul's messages. Get quiet during everyday tasks. When you're in the car, turn off the noise in your car and in your head. When you're in the shower, focus on your breathing and quiet the thoughts. When you come to a red light, close your eyes and take three deep breaths. If the light turns green, the person behind you will let you know.

You may hear the voice of guidance inside your head, as a thought or a knowing. It may be in your own voice, or in a familiar voice that may not be your own. Or you may hear the voice of guidance coming from outside you, perhaps beside you, whispering in your ear, or by your shoulder. It can be male, female, or non-gender.

Sometimes it's difficult to know if we are listening to our soul calling us, guidance giving us direction, or our ego mind messing with us. There is a different quality between true guidance and false guidance. False guidance can be your ego mind or it can be spiritual guidance that isn't coming from a higher consciousness.

True guidance is based in love. It has no story or long explanation attached. It's often just a couple of words or sentences, generally as a suggestion of what you need to do. It's very direct and to the point.

True guidance can often be a simple statement about "do this" or "don't do this." It just gives you instructions, without describing the results or giving details about how or why to do it. It is supportive and empowering.

False guidance is often based on fear, worry, or doubt. It can make you feel less than others, weakens you, or tells you that you're not good enough to do something. It is often your mind's first response to true guidance.

It may tell you why it's not a good idea to do or not do something, and it will tell you what's going to happen as a result of doing a specific action. It may give lots of details, and it has a story about why and how things will occur in your life.

When we seek guidance and intentionally listen to our inner voice, we often hear our true guidance and then immediately false guidance steps in as the next thought. That false guidance can have more emotion and energy attached to it, often fearful. It can feel urgent or make you feel unprepared or not good enough.

True guidance is neutral and has the knowledge that you can do whatever it is asking of you. "Sell the house" was guidance I received without any instructions about why or where I was to move. Inherent in that guidance was a calm certainty that I would be led to the next step when I needed that information.

True guidance doesn't mess with you and change its message constantly. I know a woman who is very caught up in listening to spirit. Her heart is absolutely in the right place. She's psychic and intuitive, and she bases her decisions on what she believes to be true guidance. The problem I see is that she gets mixed messages. "Spirit" tells her to do this thing and expect a certain outcome. So she does as told, but that outcome does not occur. So then spirit tells her why it didn't happen, and now she is to do something else, and expect a different outcome. This story repeats itself over and over, year after year.

Such changeability doesn't align with true guidance. True guidance doesn't lead you to take actions that are out of integrity, against someone else, or even against the law, such as "don't pay your bills and they will go away."

False guidance can show up in such a way that you think it is your spirit guide or an angel who gives you answers. You may think you are listening to true guidance, but the information you receive isn't consistent with how true guidance shows up. The messages could very well be from somebody who died (who you may or may not have known) and is hanging around, giving you advice about what to do and why. They are from a lower consciousness than your spirit guide. Their lower-level advice may feel familiar and be easier to accomplish. Realize that your spirit guide is also sending you messages but they may be suggestions you don't want to follow.

So how can you tell the difference? Look at the results in your life. True guidance gives you consistent, powerful, supportive, and motivational messages. They are short, neutral, and to the point. False guidance makes you shrink inside, feel less than, or give you reasons (excuses) why your life isn't working.

Remember, this is your body and your life. You are in charge of what happens. Do not give authority of your life over to any spiritual being when the results don't empower you. There are crazy voices "out there." It is your job as the owner of your body to be prudent and careful about what you listen to and follow. Not everything you hear is from a reliable source. Not all guidance is true guidance.

Beware of Ego-Based Messages

Another way many seek guidance is to get a psychic reading. While many psychics are spot on, and able to give you valuable insights into your life, others are hit-and-miss, or just plain wrong. They are the ones who speak *from* their ego and *to* your ego, building you up as some great or wise spirit. I've had numerous very helpful readings, and some real "doozies" as well.

Over the years, I have known many people who check in with a psychic for every single decision. Sadly, their lives often aren't working well. If you rely on someone else, even if he/she is a good psychic, then you cease to make your own decisions and choices. You're making it more difficult to hear your own guidance. Remember this: The future is not yet determined. If you have someone telling you what will happen, that is only one of the infinite possibilities. It is always your choices that determine the outcome.

How do you tell the difference? A psychic who is authentic and tuned into you (without their ego as a filter) will give you information that:

- Helps you feel empowered or connected to your own intuition; or
- Assists you in understanding more about your spiritual path; or
- Explains why things are unfolding as they are and it resonates as true within you; or
- Describes patterns of behavior that help you.

It's not necessarily all "good news," but it is information that sinks in as valid and helpful. Hearing truth can make you feel uplifted and positive about moving forward.

On the other hand, if your ego feels fed, and you are told you are enlightened, but your life doesn't exactly illustrate that, you might want to doubt the information.

I had one psychic tell me I was a bodhisattva, which means "enlightened one." I knew that wasn't true, as I have a fairly good sense of myself. She also said I had ascended with Mary Magdalene, and it was really hard not to laugh at that. After a few more highly exaggerated statements, I began to pray for guidance. I simply asked within myself, "Please give me an answer."

A few moments later the psychic said she had done hundreds of readings on women, and 98% of them were bodhisattvas. Aha! There was my answer. What are the odds of this one psychic only reading enlightened women? Not very good odds, I believe. The information she was telling everyone was from *her* own exaggerated ego and *her* desire to be special, rather than information relevant or true for the person paying for the reading.

For every single one of us, part of our spiritual path is to learn to discern and use good judgment about guidance we receive. It is a process of learning to follow our own intuition, guidance, gut feelings, and knowing. Guidance comes in many forms, and each of us has to learn how to listen to true guidance. The next step is to take action on what you know to be true.

This is all part of your soul's calling. Learning to listen to your own true guidance is part of the process of evolving into higher consciousness. If you can't recognize false guidance, then how can you know true guidance?

Make no mistake about this: We ALL listen to false guidance, daily. The false guidance comes from our own thoughts and limiting beliefs. It can be based on our emotional wounds and strategies that we've put in place to protect ourselves from future pain.

Our mind loves to tell us what to do. Much of this advice is based on instant gratification or delaying pain, and we can think it's our intuition or guidance speaking, but it's not:

- "Don't forgive that person; you're right and he's wrong."
- "You deserve to take whatever you can get in life."
- "Charge that new pair of shoes and worry about the cost later."
- "Have another drink, you've had a rough day."
- "Be snippy to that rude person because she deserves it."
- "Here's an investment idea that can't fail. You'll be rich."
- "Marry that person everyone approves of."
- "Marry that person no one approves of."
- And so on and so on.

Do these recommendations sound familiar?

We do things for the wrong reasons because we listen to our mind's advice instead of our inner knowing. I wonder how many marriages would never have occurred if we had listened to our inner knowing? I think that anyone who ends a marriage within a year or two knew before saying "I do" that they should have said "I don't."

And yet, even if they knew they shouldn't have moved forward with the marriage, perhaps it was something they needed to do for their soul's growth. No matter whether we listen or don't listen, we can grow and evolve because we learn from our "mistakes." We learn to listen more closely, and isn't that what is most important to our soul?

The same goes for:

- Dating (marrying) the wrong person and hanging on, waiting for that person to change;
- Staying too long in a job you knew you should have left years earlier;
- Hanging out with people you are trying much too hard to impress;
- Putting aside your true voice or wishes to be part of a group or to please your family.

In every case, look to see if you knew what you should do, but you had reasons for not doing it.

After you acknowledge all the ways you knew to not go into a relationship, whether intimate, friend, or work-related, it's also *very* important to look at all the benefits you gained by being in that relationship. Perhaps you learned to speak up for yourself, or trust yourself more, or become more authentic. There is no "wrong" relationship or choice *if* you learn and grow from it – and use that experience to be of service to others.

That is how true guidance (knowing in your gut what you should do) and false guidance (reasons not to listen to true guidance) work in your life.

Remember: It's not enough to just hear your guidance. You need to take action on it.

Our Body's Guidance System

We also receive guidance from our body. We talk about a "gut feeling" because that's where much of our intuition is located. It's not in our brain. Actually, our guidance system is in every cell, muscle, organ, and area of our body. Our entire body is a guidance system because it gives us feedback about what is going on inside – physically, emotionally and mentally.

As I explained earlier, we make up what everything means to us.

- An event happens and we give meaning to it.
- We then respond according to *our* meaning. Our meanings determine how we live our life.
- Furthermore, our body responds according to the meanings we make up.

Dr. Kim Jobst, a dear friend and colleague, has made the science of meaning his life work. In his article, "Diseases of Meaning,

Manifestations of Health, and Metaphor," which appeared in the *Journal of Alternative and Complementary Medicine* in 1999, he wrote:

> "Disease and health are commonly thought of as distinct opposites. We propose a different view in which both may be seen to be facets of healthy functioning, each necessary for the other, each giving rise to the other. Thus, disease may be thought of as a manifestation of health. It is the healthy response of an organism striving to maintain physical, psychological, and spiritual equilibrium. Disease is not necessarily to be avoided, blocked, or suppressed. Rather, it should be understood to be a process of transformation. ... The proposition here is that perceived meaning, and the way it affects how life is lived, is at the root of all disease."

If we see physical symptoms as feedback, then we can use our body as the guidance system that it is. Symptoms point us back to health and equilibrium, and they express themselves in very specific and deliberate ways.

Louise Hay first published her classic book, *You Can Heal Your Life*, on January 1, 1984. In it, she described the process of listening to your body to discover the meaning beneath your physical symptoms. She listed many symptoms, and for each one she gave the emotional underpinning, along with a positive affirmation to help with healing. She was one of the first authors to enter into this then-new field of mind-body connection.

In the 1980s, it was not yet general knowledge that physical symptoms signaled blockages in one's emotions and thinking. Since that time, however, countless techniques of healing have sprung forth based on our mind-body connection. For the most part, western medicine continues to disregard these approaches to disease and healing. But change is coming as some doctors become more open to this connection, especially as scientific research begins to validate it.

Eastern medicine has a long history of connecting disease with emotions. In oriental medicine, for instance, lungs represent grief. So if someone has a lung disease or symptoms, discussing what that person is grieving can lead to symptom relief. Or, at least, this person gains a new viewpoint of what to change in their thinking, emotions, or life to heal their deep grieving. They may still require medical intervention, but healing the emotional underpinnings will assist in healing their entire body, which includes their emotional body.

Your body's symptoms are very precise in what your body wants you to pay attention to. For example, you may have:

- A sore throat because you are not speaking up
- A stomach ache because you know in your gut what you need to do and you're not doing it because of fear – you don't have the "guts" to do it
- A headache because you are not thinking for yourself or you're letting others decide for you
- A foot or leg problem because you're not moving forward, not taking your steps

Not listening to your body's wisdom can also cause you general symptoms of stress, fatigue, anger, or moodiness.

We tend to ignore our emotions as feedback. But they are just that. And if we do not recognize them as feedback, they will likely worsen, turning into physical pain or even disease – because that's what we do pay attention to. Physical manifestations shout, "Pay attention. You're really hurting yourself. Do something about this." They are signals to bring us back to living from our heart's desires, to living with purpose, personal integrity, and truth.

I had a friend who was a very talented man. F
day Renaissance man in that he was a scientist, inve...
musician, singer, spiritual seeker, and engineer. But he c...
emotionally let go of his early childhood trauma – no matter wha...
type of healing work he tried.

He was tenacious, like a bulldog, which served him well in life.
But it was also his downfall, because he held onto his old emotional
wounds. He developed lung cancer, although he never smoked and
wasn't around smokers. And he died within a year. He believed he
had tried everything to resolve the emotional wounds, and he didn't
want to live another thirty years with that baggage. In spite of all he
accomplished, grief led to his lung disease.

I won't go into detail about the mind-body connection, because
that will be the subject of an upcoming book I'll be co-authoring
with some colleagues who are experts in this field. In addition,
there are many books on this subject. It's a fascinating field of study.

It is enough here to say that our body chooses its symptoms
with finesse. Symptoms are not happenstance or random. They
have significant meaning for each individual. We can look at lists of
what diseases mean, but it always comes down to each individual.
If you ask, your body will tell you what the symptom means. When
you ask, listen for the answer. It may show up in a TV ad, a social
media post, an overheard conversation, a quiet voice within you, or
any number of other ways. Stay alert.

For example, if you have a heart symptom, how does it relate to
your joy or love of life? If you have a shoulder problem, what are you
shouldering too much of? If you have leg problems, what is keeping
you from moving forward in life? If you have a sugar metabolism
problem, have you lost the sweetness of life?

You can actually journal with your symptom. Write down:
"Symptom, what are you trying to tell me? What do you need me to
know?" Then be quiet, and write down anything that pops into your
head. Keep writing because writing can help the words flow. Or,

hold this conversation in your head. Sometimes the message comes easily; sometimes you need help from another person to access it.

Listen to what your body wants you to know about your inner world. Your symptoms are serving a purpose: To get you to pay attention to how you are throwing yourself off-center. Your body wants you to return to full vitality and purpose. Your soul can talk to you through your physical symptoms to guide you on your path to fulfilling your life purpose.

Guidance and intuition come to you through many forms. It's up to you to become familiar with your own inner voice, your body's voice, and your higher-self voice. No one else can do this for you. Yes, you can read books and attend seminars to learn to listen more closely. But it really comes down to this: Get quiet and listen. Don't believe everything you hear in your head, because most of it is made up or just random thoughts recycling through your mind.

Be on the lookout for those times when you are touched by grace, when a higher wisdom comes through your mind and body, and you receive clear true guidance. Your body and your life will let you know if you are listening and following true guidance. You soul will keep calling you back to Truth. After all, that is a big reason you have come into this life.

5

Fear into Courage

"Stop letting fear be the one constant voice you listen to with unremitting faith." – Caroline Myss

Sometimes, I feel stuck and un-stuck at the same time. I know I have something that is mine to do. I can feel it in my soul, in my bones, and in my Being. I know my soul – my higher self – wants me to take some action. And yet, I pretend I don't know that this "something" is mine to do. Have you ever felt that way? Pretending you don't know, when you actually do know?

I'm going through this process as I write this book, pretending I don't know what I'm "supposed" to write. I believe my higher self has already decided what I'm "supposed" to write. So because I believe this feeling of "supposed to" comes from my higher self, I keep writing. These urges move me forward – and they won't let go of me.

My body and mind, however, are at odds with this urging. Both would rather take the day off, go enjoy summer in Cape Cod, walk to the nearby pond. At the very least, "Go eat something!" they both command. Yet, the "supposed to write" grows stronger, while my desire continues to lag behind.

What is it that creates this split in us between what we know is ours to do, and our desire to actually go out and do it?

In one word: fears.

- What will people think about what I write/do/say?
- What if it isn't very good?
- What if I'm wrong?
- What if I look foolish?
- What if I fail?
- What if….what if….what if….ad nauseum.

Here's what I know for sure: Fears are part of life. They occur whenever we are at the edge of our comfort zone. They pop up when we don't know what's next, when the outcome is uncertain. We're moving into new territory, so fear comes roaring into our mind, scattering itself through our emotions, and terrorizing our body. We can get physically sick just thinking about all the frightening "what ifs…." Fear can get so loud that we back off from our desires. We say, "Not now. Maybe later will be a better time."

If you know that you know how to do something, you don't tend to become fearful. Even if the outcome is uncertain, you plow ahead because you know what to do. You've done it before; you can do it again. If fear does rise up, you know it won't be too difficult to move beyond it.

But when something is very important to you, and you have a lot riding on it, know that fear will show up at your doorstep. Think about your life and the important decisions you've made. Fear showed up during those times, didn't it? You may not even remember how afraid you were, because once you followed through, your fears lost their power. In fact, in hindsight, those fears seemed like "no big deal." Right? We tend to minimize past fears when we think about the goal we accomplished.

We take fear to mean, "STOP! I'm headed into danger." Fear is instinctual. It is a survival mechanism that warns us of danger. It is meant to keep us alive. The larger the perceived danger, the louder and stronger we experience fear. It comes down to life and death on a subconscious level.

In its "healthy" form, that is exactly how fear operates. It's a signal to be careful. But how often do you think the healthy form of fear occurs in your life? Let's look at fear in percentages: What percent of the fear you experience is the "healthy" form and is based on actual danger? Maybe 1%? Maybe 1/10 of 1%? If you live in a dangerous neighborhood or have been in a war zone, then absolutely some of your fears are real and based on dangerous, life-threatening situations.

But your fear is only healthy in the moment when your life, or the life of a loved one, is in imminent danger. The remainder of the time, your fears are like everyone else's: made up and unhealthy.

Fear was never meant to move into our life, set up housekeeping, and then take over our decision-making. That's not its purpose. Fear is meant to keep us aware of imminent danger – and then move out of our life. It's like a tap on the shoulder with the message: Pay attention! Here, now!

Fearful "what if" thoughts and feelings get our body involved. We experience

- Our stomach tying itself in knots
- Our muscles getting tense
- Our heart beating faster

Your body has its own way of communicating with you. Pay attention to all the ways it is "talking" to you as you go down the fear-filled rabbit hole.

Even though your fears feel true, that doesn't mean they are true. Your fears seem realistic, but that doesn't mean they are the truth. Your fears are logical, but they may not be the whole story.

Yes, the "what if" possibilities *could* happen. But chances are that you're making up worst-case scenarios that will *never* happen. That's what our mind loves to do; it loves to make up scary stories. And we believe them because our emotions make the stories feel likely.

So switch your thinking to the positive "what if" scenarios and make those up in your mind. What good can come from taking the actions you're afraid to take? Spend a few moments and dwell on all the infinite possibilities of good that await you.

Here's another way to move beyond fear: Focus on *why* you want to do something. When you focus on *what* you are afraid of or *how* you will do something, you can become blocked. Go into your heart and ask yourself, "*Why* is this important to me?" Let your inner truth bubble up into your conscious awareness. Asking yourself "why" can lead to your soul's messages for you:

- I want to help people transform their health;
- I am meant to teach children to be resilient;
- I have to create, it's who I am;
- The world needs this technology I see in my mind;
- I yearn to help end homelessness.

Focus on your *why* and answers will come to mind on the *how* and the *what*. But if you only focus on how and what, your why gets buried inside you. And it's in your *why* that your real conviction and strength reside.

Fear is part of life, and it plays a pivotal role in your life purpose. You will never get rid of it. You can, however, learn to recognize it for what it is, use it to direct you to your *why*, and move beyond it. You can learn to not let it lead you astray, but rather use it to know you are headed into something new.

Fear Is Not The Enemy

Wouldn't it be something if fears were actually signposts that you are on the right track? Rather than stopping you, what if most of your made-up fears are really direction signals? The question is: What are these direction signals all about?

I believe it's always the same answer: Our fears point the direction of our soul's growth.

Our fears are not meant to stop us. We are meant to move through and beyond them. It is on the other side of our fears that we experience our greatest sense of accomplishment and success. And by success, I don't necessarily mean outer success or accolades from others. Rather, we experience the deep inner sense of "I did it!" No one else even has to know about your private struggle. You know, and that's what matters most on your path.

It's easy to understand the theory that we are to dance with fear, or to dissolve our fear, or to move with it as in the martial arts by simply stepping aside and allowing the fear to pass by. But, when we are caught in fear, it's as though we are in its web. The more we struggle and fight against it, the more entangled we become in it.

You can't win by fighting against fear. When you fight fear, you step into the ring with it and then you are in its territory. When you step into fear, it can feel bigger than you, stronger than you, and even wiser than you. Your fear *knows* you are in danger and will fight you to keep you safe.

I have worked with thousands and thousands of people over the past 35 years, helping them transform their limiting beliefs and understand their soul's journey. I have found that their fears – and all their limiting beliefs – were actually intended to help them…in their original moment of creation. Fear is *always* meant to keep you out of perceived danger.

The question is, "What part of you is deciding what's dangerous?"

You may think it's your adult self that is logically, or even illogically, pointing out all the pitfalls that await you. However, unless you are in actual danger in that moment, your fear is made up from your childhood. It may look real in the adult sense, but its underpinning most likely links back much earlier in your life. I say "most likely" just to allow for a few exceptions, but in 99% of the cases I've worked with, it goes back to young childhood experiences.

For instance, as a small child about to run out into the street, your mother would yell at you, "Stop! Don't cross the street!" Her fear of you getting hurt and her strong language made a big impression on you. You stopped! And in that moment, a subconscious belief could be formed that was intended to keep you alive. In your child's perception, here is the truth for you: "It's dangerous to move forward into new territory. So don't go there. Stay where you are safe."

These childhood programs get deeply ingrained in our subconscious mind and then play out throughout our lives – until we release their hold on us. In the meantime, fear can stop you over and over again. It's time to look fear in the face and see it for what it truly is: It is a signal, pointing to the limiting beliefs that were originally meant to help you – but now hold you back.

Fear is not your enemy, although it certainly looks and feels that way. *If only this fear weren't here, then I could....* Isn't that the way your inner dialogue goes? It looks and feels as though your fear is stopping you from finding and living your life purpose. And it is stopping you.

But what if, on a soul level, you have come into this lifetime to move through your fears? That would mean that the stronger your fears, the more your soul is talking to you. Your soul – the essence of who you are as a spiritual being – wants to grow and is using this lifetime, this body of yours, as its vehicle. So everything that happens to you is aimed at your soul's purpose.

Let me say this again: Everything that happens to you is *for* you, not against you. It is for your soul's growth and development. Every obstacle and challenge is an opportunity for you to grow stronger and more resilient, have more faith and trust in yourself, experience a deeper sense of achievement, and accomplish more than you thought you could.

That's so hard to agree with when terrible tragedies occur and when people have such difficult lives. And yet, from their souls' perspective, it is all for growth. And yes, some people have difficult learning curves, no doubt about it. I'll talk more about this later in the chapter on Fast Trackers, who take on way too many challenges in one lifetime from a human perspective.

Take a moment to look at one of your fears:

- What are you actually afraid of? What has stopped you from finishing a project, achieving a goal, or fulfilling a dream? Spend a moment, right now, to jot down that fear as a note in your phone or tablet, or on a piece of paper.

- With that fear in mind, you probably have thought about how much it has been in your way, and therefore it is your enemy. But for a moment, let's look at it from another perspective.

- Who have you become *because* of your fear? What qualities or attributes of character have you developed as a result of being afraid? Take another moment to note these attributes in your phone, tablet, or on paper.

- Now consider: What if you are in this lifetime to learn persistence or endurance, or you want to master the art of getting back up again, no matter how many times you fall down, or you want to learn inner strength or determination? Has your fear helped you hone these qualities?

- Or, what if your soul wants you to experience humility. Is your fear helping you keep your ego in check?

- Finally, what positive traits have you strengthened as a result of your fear? Do these benefits surprise you? Can you shift your perspective from fear as your *enemy* to fear as your *friendly challenger*?

When you see the benefits of your fears, then you can master the art of moving beyond them, and not letting them control your decisions.

Dancing with Fear

So just how do we dance with fear? How do we move beyond it when it seems so very real, scary, and potent?

First, recognize that not all of you is afraid. Part of you is grounded, centered, and knows your truth. Fear may be momentarily overriding your grounded part, but you can turn your attention inward to find that centered part. Breathe deeply and slowly as you bring your attention inside to your core that is untouched by the fear. Breathe into it. Remember this: Not all of you is afraid.

Second, turn around and face your fears. Look at each fear as you breathe deeply, slowly, with full awareness of your breath. See each fear for what it is: It's only a thought, just a couple of words. Yes, it's filled with energy and emotion, but it's actually just some words running rampant through your mind.

Recognize this fact:

Fear is not holding onto you. You are holding onto your fear.

At any time, you can choose to let go, although that certainly doesn't feel true or possible at times, does it? It feels as though fear has you in its grip. It feels as though the fears are real and true and very, very likely to come to pass.

Third, find the courageous part of you, the part that has shown courage in the past. Shift your attention from your fear to your courage. Remember a time when:

- You spoke up for yourself or someone else
- You did something you didn't think you could do
- You received recognition or were acknowledged for a job well done

Think back to your childhood when you first learned to swim or ride a bike. Part of you was probably excited and part of you a little fearful, and yet you pushed through and did it.

Think about the time you asked a girl out on a date and you were scared to death, but you did it anyway. No matter what her reaction, you stepped through your fear and did what you wanted to do. If it went well, you reinforced your ability to be courageous and go for your dreams. If it didn't go well, you still reinforced your ability to be courageous because you survived, you moved past that incident and asked another girl out.

Give yourself credit for being brave. You can do it in any moment. Boot out the fear; bring in the cheer.

I am fortunate that I love to speak in public. I come alive with a microphone and a group listening. Research shows that speaking in public is the number one fear. People are more afraid of speaking in public than of death.

Is it a coincidence that during the week that I've been writing about fear, I've worked with several clients on facing various fears? I think not. One feared reading aloud, while another stuttered when upset or nervous. These two, in particular, illustrate overcoming fear. Both of their fears began during a simple everyday event in childhood. I've found that's generally the case with most fears. But sometimes a fear actually comes from a past life. I'll illustrate that phenomenon with two other cases.

For them, as for each of us, their fears have held them back from fully expressing themselves and have been a source of panic, terror, and physical upset. And yet, as you will see, their fears have also been a source of strength, resiliency, and courage

Fear of Reading Out Loud

A fifty-year-old man called me in a panic, saying he needed a session within a couple of days. He had a secret fear that he had never even told his wife of many years: He was afraid to read aloud.

He is intelligent, educated, well read, and yet he had never been able to dissolve this fear, even though he knew right when and where it started. He was panicked because he faced two upcoming events in which he had to read aloud:

1. A meeting that week where he would be spending the entire day with colleagues reading out loud from an instruction manual, and
2. His father's upcoming memorial service where he wanted to read a eulogy.

He had been reading all sorts of books about fear, but he couldn't get rid of his dread of both events. He had no confidence in his ability to read out loud.

During our session, we went back to the source of his fear: In the ninth or tenth grade, he was sitting in class one day, feeling very out of it. For whatever reason, his mind was a jumble and he was nervous and confused. He had always been able to read out loud effortlessly, but that day, when the teacher asked him to read out loud, he couldn't put the words together coherently. After trying to read only two sentences, his teacher called on someone else.

He felt he'd made a fool of himself; he felt embarrassed and humiliated. In that moment, his fear formed to save him from ever again experiencing that same terrible embarrassment and shame. If he didn't read out loud, he would be kept safe.

By the end of our session, he had released those beliefs and emotions that had been stuck in his subconscious mind since that moment in class. As he then thought about the upcoming day-long meeting and his father's memorial service, he exclaimed, "Of course I can read out loud!" At the meeting he read a few chapters aloud and was fine. And at his father's memorial service, he read a meaningful poem and was surprised at how easily and fluidly the words flowed out of him.

Although his fear had caused him anguish throughout his life, it also benefited his soul's growth. Because of it, he has become more empathetic and compassionate to people, qualities that are very important to him. Seeing his own fears helped him learn to not judge anyone's fears.

That's how fear works. Its purpose is to stop us from doing or saying something that will put us in danger, cause us shame, embarrassment, or even failure. That's the psychological way of looking at fear's positive intent.

From your soul's perspective, your fears serve the important purpose of helping you develop and hone aspects of your personality, such as resiliency, strength, and endurance.

Nervous Stuttering

In my previous book, *Your Life's Calling: getting unstuck and fulfilling your life lessons*, I wrote about a client who had been stuttering since she was five years old. Her stuttering began when a barking dog chased her as she ran home to her mother. She was unable to get the words out because she was so upset, barely able to catch her breath. That incident was so traumatic for her that the stuttering caught hold in her subconscious mind and became part of her life for 35 years.

Medical science taught her that stuttering could never be cured, only managed. However, after three sessions with me over three months' time, she was speaking normally without being conscious of whether or not she could say each word.

As a follow-up, she visited me while I was writing this chapter, saying that she was speaking normally, except when she was upset or nervous. Then her stuttering would come back. She believed she was 80% better than a year earlier, and she realized her beliefs caused her stuttering. Now, she wanted to be 100% cured.

Anytime you continue to hold onto a fear, or any limiting belief, it's because your subconscious mind still believes this fear has a positive intent. And from your soul's perspective, you are honing skills and qualities that are essential for your soul's growth.

In her session, we discovered the remaining positive intentions of the stuttering: Her stuttering and her fear of speaking enabled her to become resilient, to not care what others think of her, and to be OK with being different. Those qualities are huge gifts for her and have helped make her the strong woman she is today. And now she is moving in life without the fear and nervousness of stuttering.

Speak Up

As I noted earlier, sometimes our fears can be influenced by past life traumas.

I clearly remember when I moved to Cape Cod in 1998. I had no money, didn't know anyone, and needed to start a hypnotherapy practice from scratch. I decided I would teach at the local adult education center. Its classes were held at the local high school in the evenings. The subjects ranged all over the board, but they did not allow classes in hypnosis or any form of alternative healing. So I decided to teach a five-week course on transforming belief systems, and I would include visualization techniques, which was acceptable.

But I had one really big problem: I had a strong notion and gut feeling that I would be shot and killed if I spoke out and taught what I knew.

Logically, I knew that wasn't true. But my emotions and my mind were going crazy. I was scared, and yet I knew it was just a past life memory coming through to stop me from getting killed.... again. I had a friend help me through that past life in which I was shot for teaching. With that lingering fear cleared, I have gone on to teach and speak at conferences and workshops internationally.

I know that when a past life is seeping through, it feels very true and real, but it makes no rational sense. Many people reading this book will have had lifetimes as healers – and been killed, hung, executed, lynched, betrayed, or any number of other life-ending scenarios. Sometimes that fear seeps through to stop you from doing what you are meant to do this lifetime.

In fact, you might have been scared off from your life's calling any number of other lifetimes because of fears from even older lives. Yes, you have been killed for speaking up. Yes, you have been betrayed for telling your version of the truth. Yes, you have been humiliated and ridiculed for your ideas in other lives.

Here's my best advice: It's time to get over it and move on with this life. Stop using who you used to be, and what you used to think, as your rationale for not doing what your soul is calling you to do. Chances are greatly in your favor that you won't be killed this lifetime.

Could you fall flat on your face? Yes. Take that chance anyway, so you can learn what didn't work, pick yourself up, and try again. Your soul is not going to stop hounding you until you become bold. So it's better to step out this lifetime and learn at least some of what you set out to do.

If you are stuck in fear, take a good look at what you really think could go wrong. What is really holding you back? And then get help dealing with it, moving beyond it, healing whatever needs to be healed within you so that you can get out there in the world.

20 Minutes

I held a four-hour life-between-lives session with a man, whom I will call Gunter. Since the age of 18 in this life, he has experienced intense stomach pain that comes and goes. For over 20 years he has visited doctors and done every sort of medical test known, but to no avail. It turned out that the pain came from a past life death trauma. As he was experiencing that past life in our session, he described it out loud to me.

"I was a happy, playful, mischievous German boy of 10 who liked to play jokes on people. My father was a very serious man who didn't seem to understand me, and both of my parents worried quite a bit about me."

At the age of 18, Gunter had a party to celebrate his graduation from high school before he left to join the German army. WWII was just beginning. He didn't want to go, but he was forced to go by his father. He knew he wasn't supposed to be in the army because he didn't want to hurt people, but "everyone had to go." (During his regression, he was very emotional at this point.) He didn't understand or like what was going on in his country. He believed the world wasn't working properly.

In the army, Gunter was friendly with everyone, and he tried to make people laugh. Many of his comrades loved being in the army, but he had a bad feeling about what was coming. He knew it was going to be really bad and he didn't want to be there.

In his first few days in the war he had not yet been in battle. One night, he was with his comrades, sitting on the ground, waiting in an empty town. They were cooking dinner, getting ready to go somewhere. He was very happy in that moment being with his friends.

All of a sudden, they heard noises, big explosions. He started running toward the sounds, gun in hand, telling himself to be brave. He was trying very hard to be brave even though he was very afraid. Chaos ensued as all the men ran in the dark and shots rang out from among the trees on the left side of the road. He was surrounded by screaming, running, and shooting. Suddenly, he was shot in the stomach; he began screaming in pain. Then it was over.

He felt his spirit move up and out of his body. He was so glad it was done. His first thoughts were, "What a waste! People are stupid!"

As he moved into the spirit world, he received help from spiritual beings to release the energy of that lifetime, especially the heaviness of his death trauma. He described it as feeling released from a cocoon, as if he had been stuck in clay when on earth.

But one last little spot of that trauma was left with him to remind him in his next life, which is his current life. That was the cause of his stomach pain (which has no longer plagued him since he relived the past life explosion). While reliving that spiritual healing, he said, "I'm usually perfect, and this is a little tiny spot that doesn't belong there. It's annoying to have this little spot."

After receiving the healing and release, he went to the "library" where he was given his book of life, which contained all the memories of his past lives. A female spirit helped him review that past life. As he reviewed that childhood, she pointed out how everyone had loved him and how happy his parents were. She encouraged him to keep feeling that happiness, joy, and sense of belonging. He commented, "That life wasn't all bad!"

As he moved forward to review his time in the army, he got quite nervous, but was encouraged to go slowly. He felt what it was like in the barracks, laughing and telling jokes, feeling happy, appreciated, and experiencing a true sense of belonging.

But he resisted going forward to the end of that life, saying, "I don't want to do this at all." He was actually amused by his resistance because he knew he couldn't be hurt anymore.

The female spirit told him, "This is extremely important for you." She kept reminding him,

> "Remember the love, being loved, being loving, happy, and belonging. Remember what these feel like. Feel the marching. You are afraid, brave, and powerful. Feel being brave. You are brave. Feel it. It's important for you to feel being brave."

As he relived hearing the gunfire and running toward the explosions, she slowed down the unfolding scene so he could feel his feelings. He was afraid, but he was still going to do what he needed to do.

She stopped the scene when he was running and asked him where his fear was. He answered, "It's in the lower part of me, and it isn't big. On my top I feel strong, brave, and determined."

As he felt being brave, he gained the insight that bravery had become part of him and is in this current lifetime. He's brave. He had to be brave in that lifetime so that he could feel it and make it part of him in this lifetime.

"It was worth it!" he exclaimed. The realization hit home that his former life wasn't a waste after all. The female spirit explained,

> "You did a good job. You have to remember you're brave now. That life was about the 20 minutes where you *decided* to be brave. You had been afraid before, but at that time, you were brave. That is what is important."

In this current life, Gunter continues learning about being brave, but in a different way. In his pre-birth planning, he saw that he only had a 1% chance of living to age 40. He was told, "you're probably going to die due to sickness." But he was confident: "I won't die." He foresaw that he lived through the sickness because of his faith that everything would be OK.

As he reviewed his past life in the spirit world, he told his guide, "I told you so; I lived!" So he is now in phase two of his life. "Relax. You were supposed to be dead at 26, so this is *all* extra," she told him. He is to carry on where he left off in that past life, making people laugh and feel happy, helping others feel lighthearted. He has already done the important work, now it's time to have fun.

His bravery showed up as faith and trust in the greater purpose of his life. He now lives with the theme of bravery every day: His last name is synonymous for courage and bravery, as a constant reminder of his life purpose.

Apply Gunter's experience to your life: How do you exhibit bravery? Look at your day-to-day decisions about how you want to show up in life. Do you give yourself credit for your bravery and for your ability to move toward your dreams and goals in spite of your fears?

Remember:

Fear will always show up when you are at the edge of your comfort zone and moving into new territory.

When you make a *decision* to move forward *no matter what,* then you can more easily move beyond your fear because you're not wasting your time and energy thinking, "Should I or shouldn't I?"

The 20 minutes Gunter spent running toward the explosions were pivotal for that lifetime. He experienced being brave in spite of his fears, and that bravery carried on with him as a soul into this lifetime. He certainly didn't know in that past life how important that bravery would be for him in his current life.

Most of our fears are not the real life-and-death situation Gunter experienced. Most of our fears are entirely imaginary and not likely to happen.

As you look at your own life, what small act of bravery could you see as pivotal in your life? When have you said, "YES!" to life and moved forward through the fear? Look at the ramifications. You can change the trajectory of your life and have totally different life experiences when you make a decision to follow your intuition (your inner knowing) and you *just do it.*

I write about fear because fear will always show up in your life. It's part of life and your soul is calling you to move through and beyond it. Do not let fears stop you, especially when the fears are entirely made up in your mind.

Caroline Myss, author of *Defy Gravity,* wrote on Facebook in July 2015,

"Act on your guidance without constantly saying that you're frightened and require proof that you will be safe. You will never get that proof. Every choice in life is an act of faith. Stop letting fear be the one constant voice you listen to with unremitting faith. Be outrageously bold in your belief that you will be guided, but do not have expectations of how that guidance will unfold. Keep your attention in present time – always in present time."

6

Divine Timing

To everything there is a season, and a time to every purpose under heaven. – Ecclesiastes 3:17

We all have had the experience of time stopping or slowing down. Some things seem to take so long to occur. And at other times we wonder how it is possible that the years have slipped away so quickly. For myself, it seems impossible that I have been doing this work for thirty-five years. Yet, during the past many years, I encountered phases when time incredibly slowed down.

In truth, of course, time never changes. Each second, minute, hour, day, and year is exactly the same as the year before and the year to come. We know that it is simply our perception of time that changes.

I would venture to say that most of us have trouble with time. We can even develop an *adversarial* relationship with time: Always rushing, always late, never enough time. We find ourselves with too much to do and too little time. Have you ever felt that time was not on your side? Do you struggle day-in and day-out with time?

Or take the opposite side of the pendulum: Have you had times when your day drags on minute by minute? Of course you have; we all have. We wish for the day to be over so that our tedium will end – and we can *live*. Maybe you're enduring this dragging-day phenomenon because you are (or were) in a job you detest, but you feel trapped and unable to leave. Or perhaps you are ill or injured, and now cannot live the active life you once enjoyed. Or maybe you are terribly stressed out and you are trying to force something to occur that just isn't coming together. Oh, to be out of these time nightmares, right?

Time is something we all deal with, and yet time is not our boss. Time is actually based on our own perceptions and thoughts. Time is neutral and constant, but our thinking and relationship to it can cause it to be either against us or on our side.

Do you fight time? Do you think something in your life should already have happened years ago? Or can you stay present to whatever is occurring and believe it's all in right and perfect timing? Most likely, you are somewhere between these opposites.

Divine timing means that there is a higher power at work in our lives, orchestrating situations and opportunities for our highest good, bringing into our lives circumstances, people, and events that give us ongoing chances to grow and thrive. It means that, even if we are unconscious of the bigger picture of our lives, our soul/God/ the Universe has a direct and mighty influence on our lives – every moment, in fact.

Divine timing brings incredible synchronicities into our lives: The perfect song playing the message that we need to hear; a stranger coming into our lives with information we need to know; a piece of the puzzle we are looking for suddenly appearing; a friend calling at the very moment we need to hear from them; an opportunity appearing that propels us forward in life.

What do you believe about divine timing, and how does it fit into your process of conscious intention and creation?

Playing With Time

In the 1990s, I had a practice of choosing one spiritual principle each year and then delving deeply into it. One year I choose "divine timing." I wanted to know what I believed, and what I experienced about divine timing.

I lived with these questions:

- If divine timing is true, is it true all the time?
- Is it possible for divine timing to be true just some of the time?
- Is there no such thing as divine timing?

I chose to believe that *if* there is divine timing, it can't be active sometimes and inactive other times. I didn't believe a spiritual Truth would be random. Truth is consistent and in effect at all times, with all people, in all circumstances. It's either true in all circumstances or not true at all.

In practice, this meant that any time I was hurried or rushed, such as when I was sitting at a long red traffic light, I would take a deep breath and remind myself, "divine timing." I would relax and remind myself, "All is well." I would take right action, such as calling ahead to wherever I was going to let them know I might be late. Or, many times, I would find I would arrive on time despite the terrible traffic.

One morning remains etched in my memory. That was the morning I began to deeply understand just how much effect we can have on time. I had read that time is an illusion, but I had not yet experienced that consciously or intentionally. It was still a theory to me.

At the time, I lived in San Jose, California, and had a forty-five minute commute to work. Every morning, the commute was pretty much the same. That one particular morning, though, I had to get to the bank before work, and I knew that would take an extra fifteen minutes.

So I did my practice: I simply prayed "divine timing." That's it, that's all I asked for. I then went about my usual routine. I didn't hurry. I just left home at the same time as always. The traffic was its same typical pattern.

And yet, I was able to go to the bank and arrive at work at exactly the same time I always did. Somehow, I had created an extra fifteen minutes. That made a deep impression on me, and gave me reason to really ponder my relationship with time.

I continued to actively call upon divine timing to help sort out matters in my life. It was my prayer and my intention that divine timing would rule my life that year, and I would be conscious of it. My goal was to decide what I truly believed.

By the end of the year, I had accumulated enough "evidence" for myself to decide that divine timing was a Truth principle that I would live by, even though I often didn't agree with or like the timing of the circumstances in my life or in the world. I still call on this principle if I'm rushed or anxious about running late, or wanting a package to arrive on time, or even just worrying about the future. Simply by bringing it to mind, my body and mind relax and I shift back into the present moment. I let go of my stress, and play the game in my mind of seeing how divine timing will show up next in my life.

It's a Dance

What I have learned since then is: How we create our lives is a dance. It is a dance between infinite Source and our own thoughts and actions. It's not as simplistic as "it's all in divine timing and it will happen as decreed" or as egotistical as "I create my reality by my thoughts." In reality, divine timing is the result of a beautiful merging of the power of our mind and thoughts, the desires of our heart, our clear intentions, and the Infinite/God/Source/Soul.

Yes, divine timing is always at work, and the more we are aware of it, the more we are able to be in its flow. That's what the expression "be in the flow" is all about. We are aligned with a higher order and we are saying "yes" to its flow. When we are burdened by stress, fears, or negativity, we struggle against this flow. We build dams in the river of life and find excuses why life isn't working in our favor.

This is the spiritual lesson of "letting go" and allowing life to lead us. At the same time, we are giving direction to the river of life by our thoughts and intentions.

The way we experience life is a mirror of our inner thinking.

If we have a clear intention of what we want to create or have in life, and we are able to focus on our intention, then the Universe conspires to bring us opportunities that will propel us toward our desired outcome.

We often get tripped up in our conscious creation and our working with the Infinite when the outcome isn't the way we want it. So we resist. We tell the Infinite, "No, that isn't the way this is supposed to unfold in my life. Make it easier, make it safer, and most of all, tell me exactly what is going to happen so that I know it will all be OK."

But that's not how the Universe works. We are given divine opportunities that will give us our heart's desires, yes. But, these divine gifts may not be packaged as we expect, so we turn them down. Maybe the opportunity requires us to change, and we're not ready to change. Or maybe the opportunity appears to be for someone else's good, not for ours.

Well, the Truth is: Whatever the Divine unfolds for us generally requires us to grow, change, and do things that scare us to the depth of our being. Yow!

This is how divine timing dances with our intentions and desires. They work together for our highest good. It is our job to say "yes" and sometimes even "YES!" to the opportunities life presents to us, in spite of our fears and in spite of the monkey-mind chatter that tells us we are doomed.

Your soul calls forth this dance of life. Listen to your heart by paying attention to what you love. Step more fully into life by trusting your passion, because it signals what you have come into this life to create, learn, and be. You, and only you, are responsible for how your life unfolds. You experience life by the thoughts you hold in your conscious and subconscious minds, as well as the actions you take, and the emotions you allow to flow through you.

A client of mine illustrates this point beautifully. She and her husband were looking for a house to buy and found one they fell in love with. Yes, it needed a lot of work, but they knew they could do most of it themselves. Their offer was accepted, but the house was a short sale, which meant there were several months waiting for all the paperwork to be processed. During this time she did her visioning and saw herself in the new house. She set her intention that it would all go smoothly. She had a gut instinct that its pool was a bad idea, but she ignored that feeling as she began buying items to decorate her new home. For all intents and purposes, it was her home and she could see herself living in it.

On the last day in which the owner could back out of the sale, that is exactly what happened. One minute she was a homeowner in her mind, the next moment she was devastated and deeply felt the loss of the home. She went through the grieving, all the time affirming "this or something better." We can know and use these spiritual principles, and still feel the effects of disappointment and other emotions.

A few months later they found another house, much nicer, and it didn't need the work. This sale closed and they moved into a beautiful home. They later drove by the neighborhood where they had wanted to buy and realized what a gift it was to *not* live there. A new neighbor had moved next door and filled the yard with old cars, beat up trucks, trash all over, and lots of people coming and going. They were so grateful to have been led away from what would have been a disaster for them – although at the time of the loss, they couldn't have known this would be the outcome.

You can slow down your creation process by being bound up in fear and not taking the actions your gut is telling you to take. Or you can speed up the process by being clear on what you want and then taking daily action.

Whether you are accelerating or slowing your own creation process, know that Infinite Source is always at work at the same time assisting you in following your soul's plans for this lifetime. Also know that Source's timing may not be the timing you would like. There is more at work in your life than just your conscious plans and intentions. Your soul's picture of who you are to be in this life is much bigger than your conscious picture. That's why your soul's plans sometimes necessitate waiting, growing, and becoming, rather than quickly imagining and getting.

Neither you nor I (nor anyone else) have all the information or all the answers about why our life is the way it is. But when you listen deeply to what you desire in your heart, you have a compass to guide you. You may be led in directions you would never have dreamt you would go: Go anyway. Your life may feel stalled and you are chomping at the bit to get going: Look inside and see what fears are stopping you, and then take action anyway.

It may very well be that your life is unfolding in exactly the right timing for you, even though it can feel slow or stuck. What if you are being prepared for a deeper level of your soul's work – work you are not even aware of? And, what if the way you spend your time until "it" happens – whatever "it" is – is vital for your soul's growth? Spiritual growth is not instant; it can take years to cultivate and deeply integrate the qualities and knowledge you need to do your soul's calling this lifetime.

Know this:

The entire path of your life is your soul's calling,
not just some outcome at the end of it all.

How you live your life, the people you interact with, the choices you make, the books you read, the discussions you have with others, and all the other activities of your day count greatly in living your life purpose. It all has meaning and importance. If you ask to see your life through that filter, you'll begin to see how divinely led your life has actually been.

Resistance as Divine Timing

What happens though, when we are slowed down or stopped as part of a bigger plan? What if divine timing requires us to go more slowly, take detours, or remain stuck in some area of our life for a time? So many times, we beat ourselves up because something we desperately desire hasn't occurred yet. We may do all of our spiritual work: We meditate, pray, take courses, journal, listen to the voice within, are open to change, meditate some more, and take actions daily in the direction of our dreams. And yet, we still end up in a place that feels all wrong, as though something hasn't gone correctly. We listen to spirit, we take a step out in faith, and then it doesn't work out the way we expect or desire.

What is that about? We expect to be successful if we have done all our work. We expect our wishes to work out when we have meditated and done due diligence with our inner work. We expect things to go at least reasonably well for us.

But what if we are stopped in our tracks? What are we to believe then? What happens to our faith and belief in this process of following our inner wisdom when it feels as though it has led us astray?

First, take an honest look at your thoughts. It may be that you have subconscious programming from childhood that tells you, "you never get what you want," or "it's not spiritual to be successful and wealthy," or even "you don't know enough yet." So even if you are taking action, your own thinking can be throwing a wrench in your creations and bringing everything to a halt.

Second, you don't know the whole picture. You don't know how this "being led astray" actually fits in as a necessary part of the bigger story of your life. What if you are being held back or slowed down for a reason that you don't know about? Perhaps you are being prepared for some work and this "setback" is crucial preparation. What skills or qualities are you learning from this "delay"? Maybe they are exactly what you need for the next phase of your life. Perhaps what you think is a detour or a wrong turn is actually a vital piece of your journey.

Here's an example: A friend of mine bought a condo to increase her grandchildren's inheritance. Worthy goal, right? However, it was her first experience as landlord and she did not check out the credentials of the first tenant who met her terms. What ensued seemed like a definite wrong turn.

The tenant was not ideal: She did drugs, was in a gang of thieves, and had boisterous arguments outside in the middle of the night. As a result of being the landlord, my friend learned new skills. She learned how to work with the police, how to hire and work with a lawyer, how to deal with a difficult tenant, and how to call a meeting with the police to listen to the angry neighbors.

She finally got the tenant out and sold the condo. As it turns out, her "wrong turn" taught her that she could speak up and survive an arduous ordeal. She's now using her newfound bravery to promote causes she believes in.

So, if you feel detoured or held back, look for the benefits of being in the situation where you find yourself. If you say there aren't any benefits, then look again. There are always benefits. In fact, because the Universe works in divine balance, you should be able to find benefits that balance (in number and intensity) the "problems" you encountered. Isn't that a thought-provoking idea to ponder?

Keep two spiritual principles in mind at a time like this:

1. Be grateful for all things, because gratitude brings about blessings.
2. We are what we think about, and our perceptions create our reality.

If you are in a situation that isn't going the way you expect, be grateful for the situation, even before you know its blessings. Be grateful no matter what, because gratitude is a high level of consciousness and energy. In fact, it is like a magnet, bringing good into your life.

Also, tell yourself that this situation is all for the best. Even ask that the blessings be revealed to you. Ask your higher self to show you how this seeming detour or wrong turn is for your highest good. Then look for that good and be grateful for it as well. This isn't always easy, by any means, especially if you are greatly challenged by life.

If you fall into victimhood and resistance, as in, "why did this happen to me?" or "things never work out for me!" or "I'm screwed again!" or "this is taking way too long," know that your victim mentality will keep you in that low level of energy. Things are not so likely to work out well for you. What you desire may continue to evade you. It's up to you. Change your thinking.

Be careful of your thoughts because they are powerful creators. If you are detoured, what were your thoughts and intentions? Did you think, "Oh, I knew this would happen! Nothing works out for me." If that was your thinking, then that contributed to the outcome. But no matter what happens, even when things don't work out as you want, you can be grateful and look for the blessings… and change your thinking.

Rather than judging yourself as wrong, slow, off track, unqualified, or any other negative perception, know that you are doing your best to overcome obstacles. Know that you can choose to believe that you are divinely led. And, in balance with that, also do your inner work to ferret out your subconscious beliefs or inner saboteur that helped lead you where you didn't want to go.

Dark Night of the Soul

At different times in our life, all of us go through a phase called "the dark night of the soul." This occurs when there is a loss in one's life, such as: The death of a loved one, divorce, job loss, serious car accident, financial loss, ill health or disease, moving to a new home, becoming a caregiver for a loved one, or any other life situation where something ends. As a result of the ending, life is different and you can't go back to the way it was. Typically, you move through the grieving and rebuilding process and go on with your life, but your life is different.

This is a time of restructuring your life, which is generally a difficult time. However, you can create a positive outcome as you figure out how you now want to live. With the loss of your job, you have the opportunity to ask yourself a very important question: "What would I love to do?" When you are no longer caught in the day-to-day busyness of your former job, the Universe is giving you an opening to listen deeply to your heart, gut, and soul, and then to move in that new direction.

If you have been caught in a financial downturn and lost most or all of your money, you may have had to sell your house, get rid of your cars and other material possessions, and start life over in a very new – and simplified – manner. You can either fight this process, desperately holding onto the lifestyle you once enjoyed, or you can go with the flow of life and release your attachment to all of your belongings and your ideas on how you thought life should be.

With the loss of health, you will very quickly come to appreciate what really matters in your life. All of your focus turns to getting well. Suddenly, things no longer matter that were previously important. What matters is regaining your health, and in so doing, how you live, think, and relate to others changes. It can be a time of great soul searching.

The dark night of the soul is a shattering of your former way of life. Your soul is calling you to take a deep dive inside yourself to see what is truly important to you. It is an invitation to change your life.

While everyone has losses and goes through dark night experiences, some people who go through an extended and deeper mystical version of the dark night of the soul. In this case, they don't experience just one major loss, but rather, they lose nearly everything. First one thing goes, then another, then another – sometimes all at once.

A mystical dark night of the soul can begin with losing your job, so you lose the financial security you once had. You may then have a car accident, because your mind was somewhere else, not on your driving. You are laid up, not able to do much for six months. On top of all this, you may get a divorce because life with your spouse has become too difficult and you've grown apart. Three huge changes. Wham, wham, wham.

What are you to do? You start over. You move to another city or state, thereby having to let go of many of your material possessions. And with your move, you lose your day-to-day interactions with your friends. Changing careers, moving to another state, and basically starting over are common in such a mystical time of change. It's incomprehensible. It's overwhelming. And it's a process for your soul's development.

This process of transformation typically lasts three or four years, or longer. It is a mystical journey that shifts you from living your life based on your ego or mind, to listening to your inner wisdom, to the voice of God, and to your soul.

With myself, and others I know who have gone through this mystical dark night, we "lost" everything in our lives except one aspect. For instance, I let go of my marriage, my home, my cats, my income and money, my job, my material belongings, my furniture, my friends, my ability to make decisions, and my way of life. But I kept my health. Others may keep their home but everything else changes, while still others may lose their health but keep their relationship.

Each of us lost some of our most cherished abilities. I had been a manager in a computer company, making decisions all day long. After I entered into the dark night, all I could answer to any question was, "I don't know." Another person who had prided herself on keeping her word began to not show up for appointments, while another who had successfully managed two companies couldn't remember to pay his utility bills.

Tremendous benefits came from going through this transformation – even though we felt as though we were losing our minds. We valued our abilities when they returned in a new form.

For me, I no longer had to know everything. I was given a tremendous gift in the midst of my time alone. As my money was running out I asked Spirit, "When will I have a job?" I so clearly heard these words, which I have lived by ever since: *You are on a need-to-know basis. If you need to know – you will know. If you don't need to know – you won't know.*

This new way of understanding divine timing has allowed me to live much more in present time and know that the answers I need will come in due time. You might like to try living from this viewpoint and see if it doesn't free you from your needless monkey-mind chatter of trying to figure out things for which you don't yet have all the information you think you need.

During your dark-night-of-the-soul time, you may feel as though a jackhammer is cracking away and dismantling the foundation of who you thought you were. But actually, it's more like a shovel turning over the hard earth so that you can plant new seeds. Yes, it hurts – physically, emotionally, mentally, and spiritually – to go through this restructuring of who you are and how you walk upon the earth. You may live in chaos, but it is not wrong or bad. It's simply one means of helping you change. Cry the many tears you need to cry. At times, you may also feel as though you have lost touch with the God of your knowing, as though you are all alone and adrift without a purpose, a friend, or a tether of any kind. One person described it as being "spiritually dry."

However, know that the truth is: You are very closely held and watched over during this journey, even when you encounter times when you can't feel it. Typically, you are guided to: Pray, meditate, go within, become silent, journal your thoughts and feelings, spend time alone, be in nature, read sacred texts, learn from wise teachers through books or on the Internet, and, most of all, listen to your inner knowing as you turn inside yourself in deep reflection.

You constantly seek to know God's Truth. What you learn may not be what you expect. This is part of the journey. You are to let go of your expectations of how things are supposed to be. You let go of your expectations for how God is supposed to show up in your life and in the world. As you let go of your preconceived ideas and dogma, you open up to spiritual revelations and truths. This is, after all, a mystical journey, a spiritual transformation. It is life changing in that you can never go back to being the way you were before.

Most of all, it is your time to let go of all the ways you thought you had to be, should be, or wanted to be. Let go, let go, and let go some more. By letting go of how you have always been, you allow a new way of living to emerge. It is a process through which you more deeply come to know yourself, your soul's desires, and your connection to God/Spirit.

I don't know why some people go through this long mystical process of the dark night of the soul, while others do not. I do know, however, that while you're in the midst of this transformation, you need to stay present to it, not fight it, and don't ask when it will end. It *will* end and you *will* come out the other side. You will be different inside. It's hell to go through, but in the end, it is well worth it, as you more deeply realize who you are and how you will live your life as a spiritual being going forward.

I'm writing about this journey because there are readers going through this who don't know they are in the midst of such a deeply transformative spiritual process. They may just think their lives aren't working correctly. They may feel as though they are going crazy. They can't make a decision. They may not have a sense of what's up and what's down. Caroline Myss' CD, *Spiritual Madness:*

The Necessity of Meeting God in Darkness, is excellent in helping you understand the whys and wherefores through this journey.

Whether you go through the dark night of the soul as a result of a single loss or many losses, be aware that you are on a journey to know yourself and your God more deeply. As you turn inside yourself, pay attention to your inner guidance, and then follow it. Take action and do whatever you are guided to do, as long as it's based in love and not physically harmful to yourself or others.

Resting Phase

Another phase, or time, of life can be called a "resting" phase. This is when you are to stop doing, doing, doing, and just be. For some, this can be just a few moments or hours in a day. If you are always on the go, constantly feeling driven to get more done, then perhaps you are not listening to that still small voice inside that may be telling you to rest, slow down, or stop for a while. Do you listen to your body when it needs to rest or do you push yourself forward relentlessly?

We are all meant to find balance in our life to stay in equilibrium. If we push too hard for too long, something is likely to break down. Most commonly, we become ill. It can be as simple as a cold that makes you slow down for a few days, or as complex as a life-threatening illness. Either way, your body is letting you know that something within your life is off balance and you need to pay attention.

I've worked with many clients who have strong subconscious belief systems about working hard and never resting. Typically, when they were children, if they were sitting down watching television or reading, a parent would give them a chore to do, right then. Or they were told they were lazy, or somehow belittled for not being busy. If these clients had an alcoholic parent, they didn't want to be in the line of fire when their parent was yelling or hitting. Sitting around made these children easy marks for this abuse. So they took on the belief that "taking it easy" was dangerous.

Other clients formed the belief that they had to work all the time to be successful. They may have had a single parent working several jobs, so they believed that's how they also had to be, just to make ends meet.

There is nothing at all wrong with hard work, except when it takes you off balance. Your body and your soul will tell you how to return to balance:

1. You'll first hear the messages in your head to take it easy, or stop working, or slow down.
2. If you ignore these messages – and many people do ignore them – then you'll receive stronger messages. Perhaps you'll have a minor injury, such as a sore shoulder, which encourages you to rest.
3. If you continue to ignore these stronger messages from within, they can turn more drastic, such as a major illness or an accident that forces you to completely stop doing.

This process can occur quickly (over a few months) or slowly (over a number of years) if you continually disregard your soul's urging: "Spend quality time with your family and friends, have fun, be social, take time off from work to enjoy your hobbies or interests, and, most of all, listen inside yourself."

One man's story perfectly illustrates the way we tend to ignore messages, even as they get louder and louder. He was working in a job that was not fulfilling, but it was employment and so he continued to work hard at it. He began to feel fatigued, and then quite drained of energy, but he ignored his physical symptoms. He then began to notice a chronic sore throat, which he also disregarded.

A short time later, he changed jobs into one that was at least a little closer to his dream job than the previous one. However, this was a high-stress position that required him to travel constantly and be away from his family and friends, so he experienced quite a bit of loneliness. In spite of that, he threw himself into his work and his life became consumed by it. After a time, he began experiencing a fever, which he ignored.

Needless to say, his body was sending him signals that he didn't pay attention to as he continued to push himself relentlessly in his job. He then had a heart attack, and was forced to take time off work and reevaluate his life. This is a common story, isn't it?

Your body will let you know whenever you are off balance. It pays to listen to it before these messages become stronger. Your body works together with your soul and your thoughts to make you aware of where you are off center, as well as how to get back on center.

You may go through a phase of several months or years when you need to rest. If you've been laid off from your job, you have time that used to be consumed by work. You can use it wisely, really taking time to listen to your heart about what you would most love to do next in your life. You can spend that time taking classes, learning new things that interest you, getting your body fit and healthy, and expanding your horizons. Or you can spend that time worrying about finances and all the possible disastrous outcomes. It's your choice.

There is also such a thing as a "rest life," in which you have come into this life to learn some lessons, but not to achieve great outcomes. In my mid thirties, I dated a man who was in a rest life. He had always wondered why he hadn't really done anything of substantial value with his life. He was a high school dropout, had worked various odd jobs, and was a talented man who wrote poetry and made music.

I had a psychic reading while I was dating him. The psychic described him, and then explained that he was on a rest life. I hadn't heard that concept before, but it made sense. When I told him about the reading, his whole body visibly relaxed. He finally received an answer that made a big difference in his life. Not too long after that, he moved away from where he had felt stuck for many years. He released his inner burden of needing to achieve and was able to get on with his life.

I'm not suggesting you use "I'm having a rest life" as an excuse for not doing the work you've come to do this lifetime. But, it can ring true for some people. It can be very healing to know that you did *not* come into this lifetime to achieve great things. You will still have your lessons to learn and obstacles to overcome, but deep inside, you know that you are not like others who are bound and determined to accomplish and achieve success in their area of expertise.

The opposite of a rest life is experienced by people I call "fast trackers." They are souls who want to move through three or four lifetimes worth of learning and development in just one lifetime. Because I see a lot of these people in my sessions, I've devoted the next chapter to talking about them, and how you can relate to their experiences even if you're not on the spiritual fast track.

Over the course of a lifetime, we all go through many phases, or stages of development, growth and change. Pay attention to whether you are letting your mind determine your actions, "keep working, you can do it!" or you are listening to your body, "I need to slow down for a bit."

If you honor your inner wisdom and your body's messages, you will be healthier in all areas of your life. It's perfectly acceptable to rest for a time and work hard for a time. There is no right or wrong, good or bad; but there is balance. It is part of your own spiritual journey to find what "balance" means in your life and to live accordingly.

7

Fast Trackers

*"Why take four lifetimes if you can do
it in one?" – Geoffrey, client*

t comes as no surprise that some clients who come to
me for spiritual regression into the spirit world have
incredibly demanding lives. They know deep within their
soul that they are capable. They are seekers on their spiritual path.
And they are doing all they can to grow and learn. Yet, they have
the most phenomenally challenging lives. What they have lived
through boggles the mind. I sometimes wonder how they can
continue to get up in the morning.

I call these people "fast trackers." They are on the spiritual
fast track. They want to accomplish as much as they possibly
can within one lifetime. The above quote sums up their thinking
nicely. I actually heard a client in the midst of a life-between-lives
session say this, in earnest. As a soul, he absolutely meant it. And
he knew he probably would do another difficult life again next time
because that's his soul's personality. Before recounting his story, let's
start with my first "fast tracker." I've changed names to maintain
confidentiality, sometimes using past life names.

My First Fast Tracker

I met Henry many years ago when I had only been doing life-between-lives spiritual regressions sessions for a couple of years. He recounted major aspects of this current lifetime:

- He had experienced four major deaths in his family by the time he was a teenager, which had emotionally crippled him in many ways.
- He was gay and had to keep this a secret, especially during the 1980s and 90s when there was still so much prejudice and lack of widespread support for his lifestyle.
- His soul mate love had died, leaving him feeling very alone.
- He was in transition, changing jobs and moving to another state.
- In many ways, he was weakened by life. To simply live each day took a lot of strength.

In the spirit world, when asked the big question, "Why take on so much in one lifetime?" he answered that he wanted to experience a "refresher" course in the physical world on moving through obstacles. He's an advanced soul who, in the spirit world, teaches younger soul students about being in a physical body: How to be strong emotionally, how to get back up when life is hard, how to overcome obstacles, and how to be compassionate.

Henry wanted to remember the energy of compassion in a physical body, so he is going through many difficult life situations that will give him the opportunity to live what he teaches the younger souls. This was his choice and, as difficult as it made his physical life, his soul's motivation was love and service.

You'll notice that he wasn't being punished for having done something wrong. Far from it. His choice was to endure losses as an act of love. By losing so many loved ones so early in his life, as well as feeling ostracized, he believed he could be a more effective channel for service, compassion, and healing. He could teach from experience on how to remain strong when going through losses and loneliness.

It helped him tremendously to understand the purpose behind so many challenges in his life. Sometimes we are unable to change situations but can live with them more easily when we know their meaning or purpose in our life. It was a huge relief for him to know he hadn't done anything wrong to account for all his losses, and that, in reality, he's a very strong soul. He could draw on that knowledge for the rest of his life.

Who knew there were people in the world who had such a mindset? It just goes to show that we really cannot know why people do what they do or why they face the extreme challenges they face.

Apply Henry's experiences to your life: If you have a life filled with challenges, what stories do you make up about why that is so? Do you make yourself wrong or feel less-than because of your hardships? How much do you punish yourself or hold yourself back from being all that you can be because you think you don't deserve to succeed, or you deserve to be punished for some reason?

You can make a decision to stop that thinking and choose to focus on the Truth. You are equal to every other person and you have just as much a right to succeed and fulfill your life dreams. You can spend your life asking "why, why, why" or you can choose to know that you are on a spiritual journey in which you are being given many opportunities to learn, grow, and expand your consciousness. It's always your choice. No matter how it looks to you, it's not someone else's fault if you choose to stay in the same cycles of your life, going around and around and around.

Have you ever experienced judging someone for not showing up in life the way you know they should or could? Probably. You're human. We all judge others, as well as ourselves. One of the biggest lessons I've learned from doing all the spiritual regressions is that we never know another soul's path. What looks like a terrible tragedy or failure in human terms can be a shining success for the soul. We just might not know what the other person is really here to learn. Rather than judging, as bad as it looks, perhaps we could be congratulating them on living their soul's plan through such a difficult time.

Characteristics of Fast Trackers

While Henry was my first fast tracker, he certainly was not my last one. I've become more aware of this type of soul personality, and when I mention the term "fast tracker" to clients who seem to fit this scenario, they instantly light up and acknowledge, "Oh, yes! That's me!" They find it affirming to be seen for who they really are.

I, on the other hand, am very much *not* a fast tracker. I can't imagine why anyone would take on so much. So my mindset differs markedly from theirs. To me, there is no race, there is no hurry, and there is no "winning." And there is no "there" where we want to arrive quicker. I'm just doing my best moving along in life. Look at your own life in these terms: Doing your best, moving along the best you can.

Fast trackers appear to have several soul characteristics in common. While we all may have some of these qualities, fast trackers tend to have them all…in excess:

- They want to achieve as much as they possibly can within each lifetime.
- They are strong souls, having weathered many difficult storms throughout their lifetimes.
- They are powerful, in that they have the ability to persevere through obstacle after obstacle after obstacle. It's not just one big challenge they face in a lifetime, but rather it's one after another after another in many areas of their lives.

- There is often an aspect of spiritual arrogance, thinking they can do anything in a lifetime. And the fact is, they can achieve far more than someone not so driven.
- They often disregard the warning and guidance of their elders and guides who inform them that they are taking on far too much in a lifetime. They have an attitude, "I can do that," even when far wiser beings are cautioning them against their plans.

As they choose their upcoming life, they may not necessarily agree to or even know about all the details of what will occur in their lifetime. Rather, they are agreeing to – and insisting upon – the lessons they will learn. That's a big difference. They are choosing their lessons – and they know some of the obstacles and challenges – but they may not be completely aware of all that awaits them.

They all confirm that we do have free will in coming into a lifetime and in planning what we will learn. We choose the lessons and purpose. We choose what we want to learn and grow through in the lifetime. This is ours to choose, and we do it with guidance and counseling from loved ones in the spirit world. We don't plan our life in a vacuum. Rather, we typically gather with those we will be interacting with during the coming lifetime and agree on the roles we will play in each other's lives. Of course, because of free will and fear, we may not show up in life for others in these agreed upon ways.

Arrogant and Strong

I've found it interesting that in numerous cases, when asked in the spirit world why they took on so much, or even too much, this lifetime, their answer is often the same: *Arrogance*. They all used that word in the spirit world to describe why they took on such challenging lives. "I thought I could do anything" was a typical response.

I also found it interesting that many of them are teachers in the spirit world. They are advanced souls who teacher younger souls about different aspects of life on earth. They specialize in teaching how to overcome obstacles, how to stay strong in the face of adversities, and how to get back up again when you've fallen down in life. So they come into the physical body to re-experience these situations to better teach other souls how to get back up again and keep going.

Ralph chose to come into this lifetime for a very interesting reason: To experience the same pain he had caused his family in his previous life. In that former lifetime:

- He was a financial businessman, a workaholic.
- He was seldom at home, and even when he was, he was not emotionally involved or available to his wife or children.
- All that mattered to him was work, and his viewpoint was that he was doing this to provide a good life for his family.
- Walking home after working late one night, he was hit by a car and killed because he wasn't paying attention. His mind was on his work.

In the spirit world, in reviewing that former life with his elders, he was asked, "Do you know what happened in that life?"

His reply was that he had wanted a better life for his family, so he had looked toward the future and missed his life. He realized that in his next life, his purpose would be to learn that "now is all that matters; tomorrow never comes." He felt as though he had failed that life miserably, and that it had been a waste.

His elders reminded him, "Nothing is a waste, for now you know. You don't know a lesson without experiencing it." This is great advice for us all.

Ralph realized he could have made more progress that lifetime, but he became stuck in a rut. Nothing would have changed because he was driven to get what he didn't have. He was emotionally cold.

There was no love from him to others. That attitude wasn't going to change in that lifetime, so he chose an early death.

As a soul, he wanted to come back quickly and have another chance to learn his lessons. He wanted to understand the pain and loss he had caused that family, as well as experience the other side of his indifference to the feelings of others. He wanted to know what they felt.

His elders recommended that he not come back so soon because he wasn't ready. They warned him, "You don't know what you're asking for. It's going to be hard. Take smaller steps." But he wanted to grow fast and he wanted bigger steps. His response was, "I don't listen to them. I have my own ability to choose. I want to do whatever it takes."

Ralph described to me how the elders looked to each other, and then compassionately at him.

> "They know what I'm asking for, and I don't. But it's my choice. I understand that I'm hardheaded, even in the spirit world. I have an arrogance about me that I can do it. It will be harder than I can comprehend, and that's OK."

His elders told him he is doing well in his current lifetime: He is remembering what he learned from his last life and he is listening to his heart. They reminded him to be careful of his arrogance because he keeps thinking he has everything all figured out.

> "I'll make a lot more progress if I'm humble. I'm proving I can handle tough lessons, but it's still a much harder path than necessary. Maybe I need to slow down some and accept what is. If I continue this way, it will just lead to harder lessons. I start to get full of myself, like Superman, thinking I can do it all on my own and that my way is the right way. Then I get knocked down."

Ralph's elders advised him that if he wanted growth, his path to progress was *connection*, rather than thinking he was separate from everyone and could do it all alone. His I-can-do-it-by-myself behavior caused him problems in many lifetimes, and he has aspects of it again this lifetime. His goal is to learn how to use strength of conviction as a positive, rather than to his detriment. He knows that if he falls back into the old behaviors of his past lives, ignoring the feelings and desires of others, he will encounter more trouble this lifetime. He's walking a fine line.

Apply Ralph's experiences to your life: How much do you have the "I can do it all by myself" Superman/woman attitude? It's a mindset that is natural for men; our culture fosters that early on in life. Women during the 1960s, 70s and 80s spent a lot of time, money, and energy breaking free of the former cultural mindset of how women were to show up in life: Submissive, ready to please and serve others, and definitely dependent on a man. So the pendulum swung to the other extreme and the desire to be an independent, self-sufficient woman was honed and honored. At the same time, men were learning to go to their opposite, which sometimes showed up as being too emotionally dependent and not honoring their strength and resiliency.

However, we find out in that's not the answer either. Balance is required: Self-sufficiency married with inter-dependence. As we grow along our spiritual path, we balance how much we can do on our own with how much we bring others into our life, open to asking for and accepting help, advice, and connection. The soul lesson may be the same for both men and women; although it will show up differently in each person's life. Where do you fall along the spectrum of "I can do it all by myself" and "I can't do it without help"?

Growing Quickly

Of course, there are other reasons besides arrogance for taking on so many challenges in this lifetime. Geoffrey is yet another client who asked for a very difficult life, knowing what he was in for. As he met with his spirit guide while planning this current life, his guide recommended, "Slow down, Buddy!" But my client was aware that the ultimate choice was his. "They don't impede our will," he told me.

He asked for many circumstances for growth:

- In relationships,
- Addiction,
- Religion, and
- Politics.

"I asked for it all," he said during his spiritual regression. "My physical body and soul won't do anything in moderation." Geoffrey is the fast tracker who said the quote at the beginning of this chapter, "Why take four lives if you can do it in one?" And he fully meant it. He doesn't plan to rest his next lifetime either, even though he knows how rough it can be.

One of his main lessons this lifetime is to learn *compassion*, because he hadn't made time for that before this life. He chose a male body so he could practice compassion from a dominant role. In one marriage he agreed to help his wife learn to get over her anger while he learned compassion. It's been difficult, but he clearly understands, "Of course it's worth it or it wouldn't have been allowed." Another relationship was fraught with struggle. He has learned that every action of others doesn't require an action from him; he can hold back and not just react.

As with other clients I have worked with, a deep "soul mate" love of his died when she was still young. Clients always want to know, "Why did they die so young?" It's often a similar answer: Their life contract was completed. Part of Geoffrey's learning is to move on with his life, to learn patience and compassion for himself, and to go on doing what he came into this lifetime to complete.

He said that during his session in the spirit world, his entire life made sense. He deeply understood that everything happens for a reason. It's a difficult concept to accept when things aren't going well, but each experience, good or bad, puts another "piece of the puzzle" in place.

A year after the session, he wrote me about one of the most important aspects of his journey.

"I have been able to forgive completely. I am not a 'hard' person but I had several issues from the past that I hadn't truly forgiven others. This doesn't mean it is always easy. We have to work at this. Forgiveness is simply acceptance! I thought, what a strange concept, but in reality it would be acceptance of something good or bad that allows forgiveness. Being able to forgive completely by understanding we all have our parts to play.... has helped me immensely and it will do the same for others who are seeking answers. If I had to give back everything I have learned and keep *forgiveness* only, I would do so. This certainly brings an inner peace."

He's doing very well this lifetime. While he's had a challenging life, he continues to meet his challenges full-on, and has made the changes and growth his soul desires during this lifetime.

Now that he understands that he is meeting his prior commitments (life lessons) he wants to go a little deeper and raise the bar. He wrote me,

"Of course I still get frustrated and have to remind myself that stumbles don't necessarily mean failure. Quite the opposite really, little stumbles most likely help us avoid great falls. The only negative (not really a negative) is I want to know more. I am being very honest when I say, sometimes I get in a hurry to finish up this life and move on to the next."

Apply Geoffrey's experiences to your life: Our choice to come in as either male or female is an important soul choice. Geoffrey wanted a male body to practice compassion, while many female clients choose the female energy to embody compassion. Everyone has their own reasons for choosing aspects of their life. Why do you think you chose to be male or female? What aspects of your gender serve you well and help you express qualities important to you?

I'm writing this section in July 2015 and transgender has become worldwide news. Olympic champion Bruce Jenner recently became gorgeous Caitlyn Jenner and, in so doing, has brought the choice of one's gender to the forefront. Looking at this from the soul's viewpoint, what might be the life lessons she is trying to learn this lifetime? What comes to my mind is that this soul, now expressing as Caitlyn, wanted to experience being true to herself and is doing it in a very public way to help shift the consciousness of the planet.

By being an Olympic athlete in the 1960s, Bruce exhibited the qualities of being male in an outstanding way. But his inner challenge was that he knew he was female on the inside, and had the courage to shift everything about his body and looks so that he could be true to himself – and become female. Caitlyn is stunning and in being so public about her shift, she is encouraging people to question gender identity. I think this is probably a big part of her soul's lessons, and she's doing it in a marvelous way.

It's my thought, however, that many of the younger children and teenagers who are now becoming transgender at such young ages may be the result of chemical exposure from all the pesticides, toxins, and endocrine disruptors that they have been exposed to. And even if that's the cause of their gender identity issues, it's still part of their soul's journey to be true to themselves and express themselves through the body and gender that feels most comfortable and right to them.

What I've learned from fifteen years of doing the spiritual regression sessions is that "mistakes" happen in life. Not everything is pre-planned and pre-ordained. We have free will and we determine the course of our life by the choices we make. We are definitely not puppets on a string, just living out some life that we chose as a soul beforehand.

When we get into the body, our personalities and beliefs can steer us off the easier track and into the bushes and tangles of life. But we can always ALWAYS find our way back to center if we go inside, learn to meditate and quiet our mind, and listen to our inner voice of wisdom. This is a spiritual practice because it takes time and practice. But it is a possibility for each and every one of us.

"Failures"

Tom is another individual who is leading a really challenging life – and it's not his first, it turns out. As we started the spiritual regression, he went into a past life where he made some choices that aligned with his soul's plan – although he didn't use those words in that lifetime.

In that past life, he was in his twenties, vibrant, had an active social life, and felt alive with exciting possibilities. He was married, had a good job, and life was great. Then his wife became sick. He quit his job and gave up everything to take care of her during her long illness. After she died, Tom felt alone and lost, and couldn't go back to his prior lifestyle because he had given it all up with his job. He was at a complete loss as to where to go and what to do.

Later in that same life, he made choices that led to another marriage. He was active in his community, became a respected leader, and was the "justice of the peace." It was a quiet life but a good one, even though he was aware of the bitter sweetness of longing for the possibilities he had given up, but content in the life he created.

As he went into the spirit world after his death in that life, Tom reviewed the key difficult decision points he had made in that life. His biggest decision was to choose to take care of his dying wife. For him, the importance of that decision was to develop character. He had a karmic connection with his wife, so he believed he needed to be there for her. At the time, though, he had been seriously tempted to choose otherwise and stay with his job. He gave it all up to follow their pre-life agreement; although he wasn't consciously aware of that agreement.

He learned the importance of making difficult decisions when he couldn't see the future clearly. As he reviewed that life with his spiritual elders, he realized he had to trust that his choices would have a positive effect on the future of people he did not know or circumstances he could not see or know. He made choices that felt best, most "whole" to him, even though they didn't make logical sense. While some of his choices may have felt small and insignificant on the human level, he couldn't know their impact on a larger scale – that is, on his soul's calling.

In his current life, Tom takes on tough assignments where it's always a little dicey as to whether he takes on more than he can manage. It turns out that he's impatient and tends to over-reach, as he has in past lives. He wants to grow in leaps and bounds instead of in small steps. He wants to be like the great and powerful beings who are his elders, and that's a "long, long, long, long process."

He explained his soul's perspective to me, saying, "I don't have time to go slowly, so I take giant steps with tough lives." While his elders admire his intense drive, they "scratch their heads" at all he wants to take on. They caution him against planning so much, but he goes for it.

In his previous life, losing it all was part of the challenge he undertook. He even agreed to take less of his soul energy and his power with him into that life, to make it even more challenging. It was as though he was running on four cylinders instead of all eight.

In Tom's current life, he has experienced numerous failures. In asking, "What am I doing wrong? What am I not learning?" he was told that it's not about what he's not doing right. It's that he's choosing to do hard work again this lifetime. In the spirit world, Tom is an effective teacher who helps souls prepare for their life on earth. He believes he needs the personal experience of failure, not just the theory, so that he can speak and teach young souls based on his having been through it. Also, these difficult experiences grind away hasty judgments. He believes that the way to be non-judgmental is to live through these experiences to be more effective in what he does in the spirit world.

He told me that he has had so many things go wrong – "stinkcronicities" – which he believes are nearly impossible unless that's what he signed up for. It's as though he's "reincarnating over and over again in this life" as he works through each period of losses and challenges in his life by starting over again and again.

It's interesting that what has made his life more difficult, besides the external challenges, has been his thinking. His life could have been less difficult if he hadn't thought there was something wrong with him. He's been very hard on himself because of what he perceived as failures. Much of his pain comes from his expectations and pre-meditated disappointments. His negative thinking is one of the challenges he came in to face.

Since he is a teacher in the spirit world, he thought he was going through the difficulties for the sole (and soul) purpose of teaching others in the spirit world. But he was also shown the influence he has made on others during this lifetime, just by being authentic, real, compassionate, and vulnerable. He has helped others on their paths in ways he doesn't realize.

In spite of how his life looks on the physical level, Tom's elders are very pleased with how well he's doing. Their final words of wisdom: "Lighten up on yourself!"

Apply Tom's experiences to your life: If you have experienced numerous failures, or what you consider failures, what do you decide that means for yourself? What story do you tell yourself about your failures?

You alone decide if you failed at something, or if you are a failure. Did you know:

- Thomas Edison had thousands of attempts, "failures," before he invented the electric light bulb (he never actually counted, so the real number is unknown).
- Abraham Lincoln went to war as a captain and returned as a private; he was unsuccessful as a businessman and a lawyer; he was defeated in four different attempts at politics.
- Winston Churchill repeated a grade in elementary school and then was placed in the lowest division of the lowest class; he twice failed the entrance exam to the Royal Military Academy; he was defeated in his first attempt at Parliament.
- Albert Einstein didn't speak until he was four and didn't read until he was seven; he was expelled from school; he was refused admittance to the Zurich Polytechnic School. Eventually, he did learn to read, write, and do math.
- Henry Ford went broke five times.

And the list of famous people who "failed" goes on and on and on. As Winston Churchill said,

"Never give in, never give in, never, never, never, never – in nothing, great or small, large or petty – never give in except to convictions of honor and good sense. Never, Never, Never, Never give up."

Dale Carnegie said, "Develop success from failures. Discouragement and failure are two of the surest stepping stones to success."

You will notice that these people failed in big ways, and they succeeded in big ways. Look at your own life and see how you have gained and learned from what you may have called a failure or setback. What we may call a failure is actually just feedback from the Universe. All it means is: Try something else, go another direction. There is no failure until you say so. Until then, it's just a step along the trajectory of your life.

You don't know the significance of your actions on a soul level. You don't have access to the impact and ripple effect you have on people, both positive and negative. Your actions, your thoughts, and your consciousness all affect others in ways you will never know. Others watch how you live and learn from you, one way or another, how they want to be or how not to be.

Feeing Disconnected

Ralene has a tendency to be strong willed and determined. In a previous life in the 1800s in the Midwest US, she defied the "appropriate" ways women were to behave and flexed her will, going against what was expected of her. Instead, she did what she wanted to do and acted as she wanted to act. She did well in that life, despite its restrictive culture.

In this life, she wanted to experience the opposite – expressing her true self, but not doing well – while still striving for self-determination through many tough years. Part of her challenge has been feeling disconnected from Source and her guides. In her spiritual regression, she learned that she has been willing to go to the depths of her own despair in this lifetime to better understand what the experience is like so she can help others who are frustrated and feel disconnected. In the spirit world, she loves and accepts souls returning home who have been in deep despair.

She is able to be with them in their despair and know it won't last forever.

She, like so many people, knows she is a capable soul and yet doesn't understand why life is so challenging. She hasn't trusted that she was on her path. She has made her current life more difficult by thinking she was being punished and believing she had something inherently wrong with herself.

One of her lessons this lifetime is loyalty. One might think, "What a lovely trait to embody – loyalty." However, she's learning it the way so many do: Through the opposite traits of betrayal, jealousy, and scapegoating.

In the spirit world, she was clearly told, "There isn't any such thing as loyalty to others. Be loyal to yourself and no one else. It doesn't serve anyone to expect another person to forego what they are called to do. Let go of your expectations. In an open and spacious way, allow others to be who they are."

So Ralene is learning to allow spaciousness, love, openness, and expansiveness in her relationships. Basically, she's learning what is hers and what is someone else's. She has beaten herself up after losing friends who "betrayed" her when she was open and authentic with them. Her guides were quite proud of her for walking away from those "friends," even though it was difficult for her.

She has also surrounded herself with male narcissists this lifetime, which has served her learning in a couple of ways. First, it has reinforced her thinking, "it's all my fault," which she is learning to overcome. Second, she is deepening her ability to understand self-centeredness. In the spirit world, when she meets returning souls, they are often consumed with themselves and their pain. To help them, she needs to have experienced self-centeredness and pain herself on earth. That's how she can most effectively understand these souls, work with them, and help them heal and dissolve their energy in the spirit world.

Being around narcissists has forced her to learn how to set and keep boundaries. She loves to give. It's her nature. She has had to learn to give only when she wants to give, rather than when she's being manipulated. She's learning the joy of giving from choice, with no expectations, versus the pain of doing things to please others, out of habit, or from force. She has found that giving from choice and love has sweetness, as opposed to feeling the barbs from others to get her to do what they want.

Apply Ralene's experiences to your life: How much more difficult do you make your life because of your negative thinking about yourself and others? Life gives you enough challenges as it is. Your thinking can add to the degree of difficulty you experience, or it can help you move through and beyond the challenges in a way that enlivens and invigorates you. It's entirely your choice. That's how life works. "Your thoughts are things, choose the good ones" is Mike Dooley's motto at tut.com.

Ralene was thrilled to learn that all her thoughts of unworthiness and having something inherently wrong with herself were all just mistaken thoughts. She realized she no longer needed to be burdened by that thinking.

What would your life be like if you waved a magic wand and suddenly all your thoughts against yourself would be gone? Breathe that in and imagine what that would be like. Ahhh, refreshing, isn't it?

For one thing, your head would be much emptier, wouldn't it? You would feel spaciousness, a sense of lightness inside. Thinking that you are not good enough or need to be punished weighs you down in so many ways, keeping you from feeling powerful and from doing all you are capable of doing.

What we do to ourselves with negative self-talk is a travesty. We treat ourselves as though we don't matter, when nothing could be further from the truth. If you really pay attention to your negative self-talk, you will notice how unkind, and even violent, you are being.

You do matter – a lot. You are an eternal spirit who chose to come into this life to learn and grow. Any negative or limiting thoughts about yourself are not true. They are just thoughts – words in your head – concepts you have made up or been told by others who made them up. And then you live your life with them as your filter – and experience them as true. They are not Truth. They are lies because they are thoughts you have been recycling in your head most of your life. Even if they had some semblance of truth in childhood, no thought from childhood is relevant now. You are thinking the thoughts you had when you were three or four or five years old. It's time to stop that thinking.

Many years ago, I had a teacher who often told students, "If I could buy you for what you think you're worth, and then sell you for what you are worth, I'd make a fortune!" Do you think that is true of you? If you have low self-esteem or negative self-talk, then the answer is unmistakably, "Yes!"

Choose different thinking and your life will change. No matter what has occurred in your life, you are not being punished. But you may be punishing yourself with your self-destructive choices.

Stop punishing yourself and learn from Ralene's experience. Make it a priority to let go of the negative thinking and begin to see yourself for the true Being that you are. This is part of your soul's calling: To be all that You, the eternal Being, can be. It's a journey of discovery to find the real You hidden under the negative self-talk.

My hope in relaying these stories is that, if you see aspects of yourself in them, you will find a new perspective. If you've been judging yourself for a difficult life, or encountering unending challenges, perhaps you are a fast-tracker who chose to learn an extraordinary amount this lifetime.

Obviously, everyone has challenges of one sort or another. So not all people with challenges are fast-trackers. Fast-trackers have a mindset that resonates within them that they want to accomplish as much as they can on a spiritual level – NOW. If that's you, you could feel beaten down and worn out, wondering why you ever thought coming to earth was a good idea.

My main point is: *Do not* beat yourself up or feel you're being punished or are inherently bad or unworthy. That's garbage thinking. Get rid of those thoughts. There's no truth in them.

No matter where you are on our spiritual path, the basic lesson for us all is: Learn to trust yourself and your inner guidance. Get rid of the stinkin' thinkin' and see yourself as the magnificent spiritual Being that you actually are!

8

Leadership and Power

"You don't need a title to be a leader." – Mark Sanborn

Are you a born leader? Do you find that you always end up in charge of projects or committees? Taking charge and leading others may come quite naturally to you, or at the other side of the spectrum, just the thought of leading may scare the pants off you. Maybe you'd rather do *anything else but* lead others.

Or perhaps you're a resistant leader, knowing that you are meant to lead, but instead, you hold back, stay in the shadows. Within yourself, you know you are not being the leader that your soul is calling you to be.

Leadership and power are subjects that come up quite often in my past-life and life-between-lives sessions. So I've learned there are many misconceptions about these qualities and the roles they play in our lives.

Often when a client tells me they resist power or leadership roles in their present life, they admit they are afraid they will discover they misused power when they go into their past lives. Well, of course they did. And of course you did. How else do you think you learn how to be a good leader and how to wield power wisely if you haven't screwed up any number of times? We humans tend to learn the hard way, through trial and error, and error, and error. And then we get it.

It's not a terrible thing to go into another life where you didn't show up as kind and understanding. Yes, you may need to do some inner therapeutic work to release guilt, shame or regrets about past life actions. But it's important to realize that is not who you are today, in this lifetime. Your other lives were all just about learning, to bring you to where you are today, and today is meant to take you into tomorrow and your next life. It's a continuum.

So who you were in those previous lives, and what you did in them, was all for your highest good, no matter what you did or didn't do. None of it was a waste. All of it can be used for good. If you were a brutal taskmaster, chances are you are not that way this time. Look at your life to see how you are currently using power and leadership. Acknowledge who you are now, not who you may have been 100 years ago.

Ambushed and Defeated

Since the year 2000, my friend Bob Olson – whom I quoted in Chapter 2 about the distinction between soul and spirit – has been investigating past lives, the afterlife, psychics, mediums, and all things related to being a spirit in a body. Prior to 2000, he was a private investigator and quite skeptical of anything that he couldn't prove or at least experience for himself.

He thought past lives were for others; he wasn't quite sure he'd had any himself. Even so, he chose to have two sessions with me, eighteen months apart. He had some most interesting experiences. In fact, he wrote about both in detail on his website, *www.answersabouttheafterlife.com/nancy1* and *www.answersabouttheafterlife.com/nancy2*.

In his first spiritual regression, he went into the life of George, a Celtic man in 1643, 43 years old, happy and proud of himself and his life. He was a leader in his village, loved his wife and son, and was well respected.

The first thing he saw in his regression was the day of a parade, a celebration, for a victory they had over the English. In the midst of the celebration, the English mounted a surprise ambush. A battle ensued in the village and many townspeople were killed.

During the session, Bob felt himself as George, and began crying, shaking, and shivering with deep inner cold. He wrote on his website,

> "It was as if I relived the horror of the moment. I was crying and I felt the dread and despair that George must have felt upon seeing his dear friends slaughtered. I suffered the sense of anguish and self-loathing that George felt for being their leader and not being able to save them. My body shook and shivered, and I froze from the very core of my being up through to the very top layer of my skin."

George lived out the remainder of that life a broken and unhappy man. Although his wife and son lived through the ambush, he took responsibility for all his friends who died and for his inability to save them.

As he released that life and moved into the spirit world, he met with his elders and learned the spiritual lessons that lifetime was meant to bring him. Bob explained:

> "I learned that even as leaders, as long as we are doing all that we can to help others, no person is responsible for the lives of other people. I learned that we do not have the right to feel in control of such a Divine responsibility. That is, we must trust that there is a bigger plan to which we may not be privy.
>
> My lesson was that I did everything I could to save my fellow townspeople that day. If it was meant to be that they

be killed during this ambush, I should not second-guess God on that outcome."

Bob also learned a lesson about forgiveness from that lifetime, especially self-forgiveness:

"My failure to forgive myself for my friends' deaths ruined the rest of my life and my family and friends' lives in relation to me. For instance, my wife and son lost their husband and father that day because I lived the rest of my life in depression and self-punishment.

How ironic that my choice to not forgive myself then negatively affected the lives of those who survived the tragic event. I missed out on twenty years where I could have brought greater joy and prosperity to those survivors as well as myself. Instead, I bathed in my sorrow and self-blame."

Bob's past life as George was not a misuse of power, even though George took on the responsibility for the deaths and let it destroy his own life. Bob is not making this same mistake again. Our regression session had a profound effect on him. In particular, it helped him understand the importance of living in the moment and appreciating all that he has, rather than holding onto events from the past.

In his current life, Bob has certainly stepped out in a leadership role in two ways in his passion and desire to help people understand that:

1. Life does not end with the death of the body, and
2. We can communicate with loved ones on the other side. His web site, *www.afterlifetv.com* has over 100,000 followers and brings hope and healing to thousands of viewers.

I have facilitated numerous past life sessions in which there was warfare and slaughter. I have discovered that when an unexpected loss of life occurs in those past lives, the client was often a leader in some way. They tended to take the destruction upon themselves, and their lives went downhill after that.

Apply George's experiences to your life: Do his feelings of responsibility in some way apply to you? You may not feel responsible for the deaths of others, but rather: In what way does a trauma from earlier in your life still hold you hostage? How do you let the power of that incident or situation dictate how you lead your life now? Or, are you feeling responsible for others, for what has happened in their life, or for you failing to show up responsibly in some way?

Know this: You have not misused power to the extent that you are unlovable, unworthy, or unforgiveable. Let this truth sink in: No matter what has gone on earlier in your life, you deserve love.

If you are holding yourself back from being a leader, from stepping out into the world with your positive message of hope, healing, or inspiration, then take a look at your thoughts and fears about being a leader.

If you think, "I'm not afraid, I just ...," then you have reasons for not stepping out.

I would ask you to stop. Take a breath. And go back inside on a deeper level. Ask again. What are you really afraid will happen if you show up in a powerful leadership role? If your answer is, "I don't know how," go back inside again. That's not the truth. You do know what to do – at least the first step, and that's all your soul is asking for.

Keep going back in and asking, "What's really holding me back?" until you get the real answer. You will get an answer. And you will feel it in your body, because your soul speaks in feelings.

As a leader, you are most likely not called to save the entire world. Rather, it could be that you need to have an honest talk with a colleague, a supervisor, a friend, or your spouse. It can be something very simple, such as telling the truth rather than pretending something is OK when it is not. That's showing leadership and using the power of truth and your voice to make a difference in your life and the lives of others. And from telling that simple truth, more doors may open that you would never have known about had you not taken that first step.

How can you show up as a leader? What is yours to do, say, or be?

If you already are in a leadership role, how are you doing? How wisely are you using your power?

Power Hungry

John was a capable, powerful, and wealthy businessman in the 1930s. He described his mindset as, "I take what I want. I do what I want. And I want to control more." He was involved in crime, guns, alcohol, and contraband. He was part of the mob and helped enforce the mob's rules. "I wanted to be somebody and this was a quick route."

He had no family, because he felt that life style was not for a family. Power and wealth were all-important to him. He lived with constant threats to his life and had to watch his back.

He died at age 59, in poor health, weak, frail, and burned out. He was alone and felt spent, sad, and empty. There was nothing for him at the end of his life. As he left his body at the time of his death, his first thought was, "What a waste. I got corrupted."

As you read this about John, you may have some judgmental thoughts about how he was a bad person, how he should have been punished, how he was off his spiritual path, or, indeed, what a waste his life was. You may even think there should be some sort of "pay back" or spiritual judgment. That's our human "an eye for an eye" type of thinking: There should be punishment for bad behavior.

But John experienced something quite different in the spirit world as he met with his spirit guide during our session. His guide, whom he called Alan, was full of love and was dedicated to him.

John described Alan as wise, patient, forgiving, understanding, and full of humor. And John perceived that Alan was actually smirking and was truly proud of how John had led his life.

What surprised John was that he himself was aware that his former life was all good, all OK, all forgiven, and all washed away. His guide described it as a "pretty colorful life." John rode through life on the edge; it was never dull.

So what was John trying to learn by being corrupt and power hungry? First, he got the clear message: "Sins, like fowl, come home to roost." He didn't think longer term. He learned that his actions did eventually catch up with him. He used his power in reckless, hurtful, selfish ways. He didn't think of others and didn't take accountability for his actions.

In that life, John wanted to learn about using power. He wanted to experience selfishness, living for now, and having a quick fix for problems. He did learn how power felt and he learned to wield it against others. But he was numb to the impact his actions had on others, because that would have weakened him. He didn't intend to live a long life, so he planned to go out in a blaze of glory without getting old.

He experienced power and strength in his younger years, but he also experienced being a frail old man, alone, and having achieved nothing of value. It became very clear to John: "I had short-term thinking. I led a one-dimensional life, and it was not the best use of a life."

John's current life is diametrically opposite to that former life. He is now a family man, devoted to his wife and children, and involved in healing and transformational work. He is passionate about helping people change their thinking, create a life of their dreams, and see their lives from the spiritual point of view. He is doing all he can to be real, vulnerable, and authentic.

Whereas he was relatively fearless in that former life, in this current life he has had to overcome the fear of "coming out spiritually." He has needed to develop confidence in himself and in his ability to make a difference in others' lives.

This lifetime he is supposed to learn to use power responsibly – and he is doing very well with this lesson. He was told he can find great joy and satisfaction when he uses power well – a skill he is developing.

His elders warned him that power is intoxicating. It could give him license to be reckless and go to excess and extremes. They reminded him that power, if used selfishly, is fleeting and has no real worth.

One of the ways John has learned about power in this lifetime is during the financial failure of his business. He had felt invincible and bulletproof, and thought he couldn't fail. Having his business seized by creditors taught him to learn to forgive those who used power against him, because they did what they needed to do. That important lesson was for his spiritual growth, as difficult events often are. His guide recommended that he "shake it off and leave it behind."

In discussing why he chose to come in as a male this lifetime, he said, "Because it's a power position." In many past lives, he has gravitated to power. In this lifetime, he wants to experience having so much inner power that he can give freely to others, so they can also lead, play, and grow. For him, the ultimate expression of power is to give it away, like leading from behind. "There's no loss and no harm done if you give power away," he says. "It's being super rewarding and super rich!"

A well-known saying is:

"With great power comes great responsibility."

These two past life stories illustrate two sides of power and responsibility. George was the leader and felt responsible for the lives – and deaths – of his village friends. John, on the other hand, felt no responsibility for the lives and deaths of those he dealt with.

He wielded power to benefit himself or his mob bosses, without regard for its effect on others.

Apply John's experiences to your life: How do you use power responsibly? Do you use your power in service of others or to improve only your own life? Perhaps you use your power against others, to get them to do what you want. When are you numb to the effect of your actions on others?

There are degrees of right use and misuse of power. One client, in speaking about her past life, said, "My desire for power sometimes overshadowed my sense of responsibility for what was sacred. I didn't misuse my power, but it was an attraction for me all the time. I liked the power and lacked humility. The way to have true power is to not be focused on having it."

Look at the ways you help others feel powerful, and in so doing, you also benefit. To be of service to others may be one of the greatest ways to become internally powerful.

Perhaps you use your power in a sly, covert manner, as this next story demonstrates, rather than in an overt manner and through brute strength.

The Charming Spy

Women come into lives to learn about power, but often in a different way than men. I've worked with several women who have similar stories to Hilda. Hilda, a sophisticated, beautiful woman, was in her late twenties during World War II. She was also a British spy. Her assignment was to gain access to a general in Germany, charming him to fall in love with her. She played her role well, and obtained valuable German information, which she passed on. She used her sexual power to entice the general – even though she had no feelings for him.

But Hilda was caught, her notes were found, and he accused her of betrayal. She was killed and, as her spirit was leaving her body during our session, she worried about not having learned her lessons because she had been caught.

She was therefore surprised in the spirit world to learn that she had done a good job. She wanted to learn to feel power as a woman, which she accomplished. However, she was almost heartless. She had buried her own emotions and was disdainful of love. In closing down her feelings, she went a little overboard. That attitude cost her a lot: No love and no feelings.

Hilda had many past lives as a male with power. As a female, she was trying to learn to balance power, love, and integrity. She realized there actually was a man she had loved in that lifetime, but she chose her job and her lust for power over being with him and leading a normal family life.

Her elders told her that she underestimated her capabilities by not taking the risk to feel more. She could have lived with love rather than feeling disdain. She learned that power doesn't have to come in the form she experienced – using it as power over others to get what she wanted.

In her current life, Hilda is leading quite a different life, and she is determined to allow love to flow in and through her. When she had her session, she was working through her disdain for men in challenging relationships, and was learning to balance relationships with taking risks. She knew she was supposed to learn to trust and get close to people without becoming overly attached.

Since her regression, Hilda has made major changes in her life. She went back to school and got a degree in Marriage and Family Therapy, perhaps, "to really perfect the love thing." She's in a very happy and healthy relationship now. And she wanted others to learn how to find their own lasting love and healthy relationship, so she has written a book on finding lasting love.

She's using her power in beneficial ways this lifetime. She can stand on her own as a female. As a healer, she is intent on showing love and caring to others so their lives are not so hard.

She's doing very well this lifetime and her elders are pleased with her progress.

Apply Hilda's experiences to your life: Notice the ways you use your power to get what you want. We all use power in different ways, and some are highly beneficial. You can use your power to lead people into their truth, or to be of service to others, or to make changes in the world. You can also use your power to manipulate and control others to do what you want them to do, regardless of the effect on them.

Look closely at your perceptions about power and how you demonstrate it. You have external power, that is, getting others to do your bidding. You also have internal power, which is your ability to dig deep within yourself and make decisions and take actions from your intuition, your gut, your soul's calling.

Within your inner power is your endless supply of confidence, integrity, strength of character, determination, endurance, persistence, and knowing. How do you exhibit these strengths, and how do you deny them?

Right Use of Your Power

Men can come into a lifetime of leadership to learn how to wield power wisely rather than by being overpowering, overbearing, or using aggressive force. A female may want to learn to use power by breaking through a glass ceiling or doing things not normally expected of females in society.

Your soul is calling you to pay attention to how you use both your inner power and your external power. Both are necessary forces in this world, and neither is inherently good or bad. How you manage both kinds is an important aspect of how you live your life.

Social media has now enabled people to use their leadership skills in entirely new ways. You can post information to campaign for or against a cause or a belief. Never before have ordinary, everyday people (as opposed to only acknowledged leaders or experts) been able to use the power of technology to reach hundreds, thousands, and even millions of people around the world – at times within just a few hours.

What you post or share can affect others in ways you cannot imagine. Someone can read what you've written or shared and gained a new insight or been uplifted in a significant way. I believe we all can use the power of our voice to make a positive difference in the world.

The truth is: We all exercise power and leadership every day – maybe in small ways, as in deciding what we will do for the day, or in large ways, as in making decisions that affect the lives of others. We use our *power* to follow through on our word, to show up on our commitments. We use our *leadership* to encourage or support others – perhaps as simply as smiling at a person standing in line, or making a kind or uplifting comment to someone who seems down. We may devote our lives to a cause that is near and dear to our heart, or we may volunteer to accompany a friend to an appointment.

If you are called to be a leader, you will know it in your heart and soul. If you are called to make a difference in this world – and by the way, we all are – be the person who makes a difference. Even small acts of power and leadership can have huge effects in the lives of others and can yield great outcomes. We don't know the higher purpose that each day brings, so we suit up and show up, as the saying goes.

Take a look at your life and notice how you use your power and leadership skills to help others improve their lives. Because there is so much corruption, it's all the more important that those on their spiritual path, those with integrity and a desire to improve the world, speak out. It's time to lead, to say what you have to say, and do what is yours to do. We need more voices out in the marketplace telling the truth rather than marketing lies.

Have no doubt that your life gives meaning and purpose, value and depth to others. It's no small thing to help another person. It's actually huge and a right use of leadership and power. Just notice how uplifted you feel after you help others. That's your soul saying, "Good job!"

9

Addiction and Connection

"We are like islands in the sea, separate on the surface but connected in the deep." – William James

ddiction and loneliness are themes that come up regularly in my hypnotherapy sessions. Because they are so widespread, I wanted to address them from the perspective of what our soul learns through these tough situations.

There is fascinating new research on addiction. Yes, it's true, a chemical change in the brain actually occurs when someone is addicted to something. And yes, it's also true that we crave more and more of our drug, whatever it might be, and we become less and less satiated.

But the big question is: What causes someone to develop an addiction in the first place?

Addiction is defined as having two components:

1. Obsession – You are preoccupied with your drug of choice, and
2. Compulsion – You feel a strong, compelling urge to have your drug.

Put another way: You've gotta have it!

We have been told that the craving and constant need for more of the "drug" that underlies addiction comes from getting hooked on it. Our brain gets hooked on the response the drug creates, so we crave more and more.

The research to back up this theory came from putting a rat in a cage with two water bottles – one full of plain water and the other laced with cocaine or heroin. The rat preferred the cocaine/heroin water and each time this experiment was repeated, the rat became addicted.

Johann Hari, in his book *Chasing the Scream: The First and Last Days of the War on Drugs*, writes about the history of the war on drugs that has been going on for 100 years. As Hari notes, in the 1970s, Dr. Bruce Alexander, a professor at the University of Vancouver, performed a different experiment. He realized the rat was alone in that cage, with nothing to do but drink. So it drank the drugged water and got high, and Dr. Alexander wondered if perhaps its aloneness was a component that led to its addiction.

So he put rats into a "Rat Park." As Hari writes, "It is a lush cage where the rats would have colored balls and the best rat-food and tunnels to scamper down and plenty of friends: everything a rat about town could want." Alexander also had the two water bottles, one with plain water and one with cocaine/heroin.

The results were astounding. While the rats tried both waters, not knowing what was in them, not a single rat preferred the drugged water. They drank only one quarter of the amount as the solitary rat-in-a-cage, and none of them became heavy users. All 100% remained non-addicted! That goes against everything we've been taught about drug use, doesn't it?

So Dr. Alexander did another set of experiments in which he left rats alone in cages for 57 days, during which time they all became heavy drinkers of the drug water. He then took them out of isolation and put them together in the Rat Park.

Again, the results were astounding. The rats seemed to go through some twitching of withdrawal as they stopped their heavy drug use, but then they went back to living a normal life, playing with the other rats and drinking more of the plain water.

For these rats, addiction was not about their brain being chemically hijacked; it was about their cage, their living environment. Their addiction developed from their lack of connection and bonding. As a member of the animal kingdom, we are innately born to bond and connect with others.

This explains, in part, why people who have major surgery and are on morphine for days or weeks after the surgery are able to leave the hospital and go back to their normal life non-addicted. If it's true that their brains get hooked on drugs, they should stay addicts. But no. These medical users just stop using it and go on with their lives. Their cage, their life, is what saves them from being addicted.

There are critics of Johann Hari's work, stating that he doesn't talk about the years of research into the changes that occur in the brain as a result of exposure to addictive substances. As with most things, the underlying cause of addiction isn't an either/or but a both/and situation. Bonding and environment, as well as neurotransmitters and physical brain changes, play a role in addiction.

This work does bring to light a very important message: We are meant to bond and be involved in community. If we don't have the bonding we need and desire with people, then we may very well turn to substances for bonding.

Loneliness

How does addiction play a role in your soul's journey? That question will offend some, I'm quite sure. You may think, "I'm not an addict! I don't do drugs!"

Here's the truth: We all have elements of addictive behavior in our lifestyle. It may not be drugs or other addictive substances.

It may be activities, such as being a workaholic, or a couch potato watching television all day, or being glued to the Internet to excess. It may even be a "healthy" version of addiction, such as working out for hours every day or volunteering on too many committees.

In the broader sense, addiction can include far more than the typical self-destructive behaviors we think of, such as excessive eating, gambling, drugs, alcohol, smoking, working, and sex.

Think about addiction from these perspectives:

- You may be a "volunteer junkie" if you volunteer for yet another project or committee, even when you are already stretched to the limit.
- You may feel driven (addicted) to do a certain behavior, whether it's saying "yes" when you want to say "NO" because you don't want to offend the person, or checking your smartphone for texts and messages every five minutes.
- You may do something habitually and feel powerless to *not* do it.

Bring to mind a personal addictive behavior, or think about the behavior of someone else (if you can't yet see one of your own). Notice if or how that addition relates to a lack of connection or a desire for bonding.

Feeling alone is a social problem of epidemic proportions these days. Research shows that the more we engage in electronic communications, the more we tend to feel alone. If we are all communicating more with others electronically, you'd think we'd feel more connected. Not so.

Albert Einstein looked ahead to this time when he said, "I fear the day that technology will surpass our human interaction. The world will have a generation of idiots."

Far too many people spend hours and hours each day in front of a screen playing games or perusing the Internet. Look at the percentage of your communications through Facebook or other social media, as compared to face-to-face. Kids today even use their electronic devices to chat with their peers sitting two feet away!

We feel alone and so we bond with whatever is available, whether it's our computer and smartphone or food and alcohol. In fact, lonely people often go to the hospital emergency room late at night even though there is actually nothing physically wrong with them. They just want company, someone to talk with them and reassure them that they are not alone in the world.

Loneliness is actually a spiritual issue. The sense of being separate is an existential experience when we feel cast out of "heaven" and on our own, trying to make meaning and sense on planet earth. And we can feel as though we are on our own, even when surrounded by loving family and friends.

In one sense, we are alone. We are each on our own soul's path. No one else's path is like ours; each of us is unique. Others certainly join us along our journey, but no one else can live our path for us, or as us, or even with us. We have each chosen to come here for reasons known to our soul, but those reasons are often hidden from our consciousness.

Our biggest problem is that we feel cut off from ourselves, and that feeling of aloneness and separation can cut us to our core. We create such a strange dilemma:

1. We are unable or unwilling to love ourselves and to recognize the true essence of who we are.
2. So, we go out into the world looking through this "I'm disconnected, I'm lonely" filter.
3. And because that's how we think of ourselves, that's what we project to the world.
4. So that's what we absolutely experience in our life.

And we think this is the real us. It is not.

We cause ourselves to experience loneliness by our thinking. It's not because of the outside world, or our family, or any other reasons. We are the cause, and the solution, of loneliness. By changing our perceptions and the stories we tell ourselves, we can change how we experience life.

Loneliness has come up many times in clients' spiritual regressions as a path of learning. For some, the loneliness was meant to be a positive situation so the clients could be free in their own thoughts and perceptions. Close friends and family members did not intrude on their daily lives so they experienced more freedom in their alone-ness. It was *not* a cold, dark, heavy state of being alone and rejected, but rather a state of being they embraced.

Other clients have had the opposite experience of loneliness in past lives, as well as this life, and have suffered greatly because of it. They desperately wanted to connect to others, to feel included, and experience a sense of belonging. Often, the loneliness came from their loss of someone they deeply loved. Rather than move through the grieving process in a healthy manner, reaching out to friends, and staying connected, they decided to close off their heart and mind to the possibilities of love and connection. They often lived out their life alone, bitter, and empty, never realizing they were doing it to themselves.

At the end of their life, in the spirit world, they could look back to see the possibilities of love and connection that they had ignored or discounted because they were locked into their loneliness.

Fear of losing love again has also been a common theme among those who chose to remain alone, and lonely, after the loss of love. Other clients focused on material wealth or security, rather than on people, and paid the price by being distant or excluded from family and even society. Many turned to addiction, primarily alcohol and drugs, to fill their emptiness.

The main thing to remember about loneliness is that we do it to ourselves by our thoughts and perceptions, and by the decisions we make. We choose to close off our heart, remain bitter or disillusioned, and stay distant.

The good news is: We have the power and the ability to open our heart and learn to feel included. Connection and feeling a sense of belonging are two important qualities we learn on our spiritual path. Each of us chooses how to learn them.

Learning from Addiction

Since addiction of any kind is a difficult way to live, why would you sign up for such a journey? This is Edward's story, which unfolded during a hypnosis session in which he went into a past life, through his death, and then into the spirit world. In deep trance, he gained an understanding of his soul's journey through addiction.

Imagine yourself as a black slave in the 1850s. You are a quiet man in your late twenties who works long, hard hours at physical labor. You're strong and capable, yet considered nothing more than property, owned and oppressed by a cruel and ruthless man. You're a good man, kind, loving and protective of your wife and daughter. You live in a shack by the master's house. Life is hard and yet there is a lot of exciting talk of freedom happening soon. You want to be on your own, building a life for your family, no longer subject to the whims of your owner.

And then the unthinkable happens. Your wife and daughter are brutally murdered by your owner. Your wife fought back when he tried to rape her, so he killed them both. There was nothing you could do to prevent their deaths.

Imagine yourself in this scenario. What happens to you after that? How do you respond to life and continue on?

After the brutal deaths of his wife and daughter, Edward was alone in the world. Freedom came to the slaves, as he had heard it would. He was free, no longer the property of his former owner, but he was still enslaved, working like a slave and paid very little. He was free, but he was alone.

Edward went into alcoholism to escape his emotional pain and loss. He was filled with resentment, anger, and rage at the owner, at the cruelty of others, and at life itself. By age 42, he was in poor health, his face was bloated, and his breathing difficult. He literally drank himself to death. His last thoughts about his hard life were, "What a waste."

Knowing that we choose each life to learn lessons, what lessons might Edward have chosen to learn in that lifetime? To see his lessons, you can look at his life circumstances in an objective manner to see how they could be the set-up for a chance to grow and develop different qualities.

In meeting with his spirit guide in the afterlife during our session, Edward judged himself harshly for that life. His guide, on the other hand, did not judge him; he thought Edward had done the best he could. That life served the purpose of Edward gaining insights into cruel people and into being oppressed, as well as to fully experiencing human conditions.

He was supposed to learn compassion for others who weren't good or kind, but unfortunately that didn't happen. Edward got lost in his resentment, anger, sadness, and losses. His intentions for that life were good – to overcome a lot – but he lost himself in alcohol. He chose to drink to run from life and escape his losses rather than face life on life's terms and move on. He could have used his newly acquired freedom to create a new life for himself. Because of the alcohol, though, his guide couldn't get through to him and offer support or guidance once he had been freed.

An interesting aspect of a life review, such as Edward received in our session, is that many of the injustices are not part of a person's pre-life plan. They result from others' free will. In Edward's case, the owner's free will led to Edward being treated cruelly, such as being whipped. The viciousness of his wife's and daughter's deaths was also not planned. Yes, their deaths were planned so that he could learn to deal with loss and grief – and then continue to have faith in life. But the viciousness of the attacks dealt too deep an emotional blow for Edward to recover. He sank into the spiral of resentment and alcoholism.

In our session, Edward discovered that he had chosen too much for that lifetime. When asked why, he reported:

> "I'm stubborn, brave, and think I can handle anything. I try to do too much in lives. I didn't take soul friends with me for support because I thought I could handle it alone. I made it harder on myself because of the alcohol. Although I thought the alcohol made it easier, that wasn't the truth."

In his current life, alcohol is once again playing a role. In this life, however, Edward is a female, and has gained support from Alcoholics Anonymous. She is learning a valuable lesson: What I think is harder is often the easier way.

With AA, she's learning to accept help from others without becoming dependent on them. She also is giving and receiving a lot of support, as together, they help one another fulfill their purposes.

As a result of her former life, she has learned to have compassion for herself, which is an important aspect of her growth. During her life review, she learned that in this life she's doing much better, especially in trusting her gut feelings. Also, she needs to keep humility in mind, for that's when blessings come. And although she has more compassion this lifetime, she is still sensitive to others' criticisms of her. She needs to overcome her resentments and be kind and compassionate with those who were cruel to her in that past life, which isn't her first instinct.

Her elders are pleased that she has chosen greater understanding and compassion rather than destruction. She knows how to heal herself, taking time to meditate and bring light throughout her body.

She again has chosen a lifetime of addiction to learn faith in herself, in God, and in others. Getting and staying sober requires connection, which she lacked in her past life after the loss of her family. This lifetime, she's making the effort to connect with others to gain support and not face her trials alone. She's learned she can't escape reality and run from her problems with alcohol.

Apply Edward's experiences to your life: What do you use to run away from discomfort? It doesn't need to be a substance. It can be worry, or letting your mind go wild with scary, yet unlikely, scenarios. Fantasy can take over and, at times, become a nightmare. If this is you, know that when you have worry and nightmares, you have taken yourself out of the present moment – and away from whatever you don't want to experience.

We all have our favorite escape routes. The spiritual practice out of escape is to remain in present time. If you've done any spiritual reading at all, you know about this practice. Stay present to whatever you are experiencing. Stay with your breath. Notice what you're noticing. And breathe some more. It's a simple spiritual practice. But it's not always easy, is it? When you've been triggered or upset, the natural inclination is to leave either physically, emotionally, mentally, or in all three ways at once.

As part of your soul's calling, consider deepening your practice of presence. Wherever you are in your ability to stay present, up the ante, take it deeper. Become even more aware of your thoughts, your physical sensations, and your emotions as you remain present to whatever is going on in your world at the moment.

A Dancing Drunk

Kathy was a farm girl in Vermont in the early 1800s whose life was filled with hard work and daily chores. Her joy came from singing in the church choir. She had a happy, joyful spirit, so she felt constricted in the very religious, puritanical, reserved family where underlying anger was palpable.

By the age of 23, she left the farm and moved to a city, where she worked in a fabric and clothing factory. She lived life loudly outside work, dancing, drinking, and having fun. She easily left the farm because she wanted freedom and joy, and she knew she'd never find those at home.

Fast-forward to age 56. She is married to a wealthy husband, enjoys a life full of friends in "high society," and has lots of fun. For her, fun equates to drinking and parties. She doesn't know if she ever loved her husband and she describes herself at that age as a total drunk.

Her last day in that life is at age 78, feeling sad about her life ending. She had never gone back to visit her parents because she had wanted to forget that part of her life.

As she entered into the spirit world, she moved into a "warm golden tear drop" essence where she received healing and energetic "patching up" to come back to herself. She told me during this regression that her energy looked as if she had just come back from a war.

When it was time to go before her council of elders, Kathy was a little reluctant because she was afraid she had really messed up that lifetime. But to her surprise, her elders were laughing and loving, happy to have her back. She realized an important lesson: They love her and she really can't do anything wrong. It was freeing for her to realize she's loved regardless of her actions.

She learned that, in that lifetime, she was supposed to have spoken up about the amount of hard work she was doing on the farm. Her brother, who was also into having fun, hadn't been helping on the farm, so much of the work had fallen on her shoulders. Her learning was to speak up.

She was supposed to have joy and to sing. She was also meant to learn to trust that if she did what was in her heart, which was to sing, then other options and situations would have opened up for her. Plus, her family would have supported her.

She questioned the elders about how to make different choices when it seems impossible. Their response: "You just move toward it, and you listen." So much work and responsibility on the farm distracted her from listening. Her before-life plan had been hard work to make her strong so that she could live in her joy.

A major purpose in that life was for Kathy to listen to herself and trust. She had a chance when she moved to the city. She needed to use her hard work as background and to focus on her joy. Instead, she just played. She would get really drunk and sing, thinking that filled her soul. She learned that was the wrong approach.

Her elders had a profound message for her: *The joy fills your soul, while the fun fills your time.*

Kathy wanted to escape that lifetime. She escaped from the farm, and then she escaped into drinking. When she was sober, she would share a lot of wisdom and love. Then she would escape again.

She learned that as a soul she still has important work to do. She needs to listen to her heart and stop getting distracted. She missed an opportunity for real love as Kathy because there was a man she knew who was a piano tuner who could have shown her real love.

In her current life, she is again female and has similar lessons. But she has not brought alcoholism or addiction into this life. She is still learning to listen to both her body and her heart, and she teaches others to do the same in her healing and body work. She realized as a soul that she had escaped from hard work in her past life, so this lifetime she is working hard.

The irony is that her elders counseled her: "Stop working so hard. Don't take it all so seriously and it won't be so hard." To make life easier, she is to enjoy her work and also enjoy play, beauty, and fun. She was told to "love yourself and play for joy, not for distraction."

With addiction, people do not set healthy boundaries for themselves. That's what creates trouble. Kathy is learning to set healthy boundaries this lifetime, both with herself and others, which she didn't do well as Kathy.

In this life, she has been given opportunities along the way to recreate the "mistakes" she made as Kathy. She has successfully avoided them. This is a good life and she learned a lot of what not to do from reviewing her life as Kathy. She is also very grateful for all she went through in that life.

Apply Kathy's experiences to your life: In what ways do you listen to your heart and your body? We can all use our heart as a barometer for leading us into what we are meant to do this lifetime. Our heart doesn't lie to us the way our thoughts do. If it's true that we are all meant to follow our bliss, as Joseph Campbell so wisely wrote, is that true of your life?

People often say to me, "But I don't know what I love. I don't know what I'd like to do with my life." I respond by saying,

"I actually don't believe that you don't know. Everybody comes into life with a dream, with a plan for what they want to be and accomplish. Remember this: Everybody has a dream. If you don't know what yours is, then it's time to start listening to your heart and body."

Wholeness

The way out of addiction or loneliness is to go inside yourself and do the necessary inner work to find your wholeness. Your wholeness is always intact. It just may be buried beneath layers of false thinking and wounding experiences. But in your soul, you are not broken and there is nothing to fix. Your soul is always whole.

Addiction is a pathway back to wholeness.

What? Think about that for a moment. How in the world can addiction be our pathway *back* to wholeness when it is so destructive for everyone concerned? Addiction can tear a person apart, separate loved ones, and destroy friendships, jobs, health, and lives.

But, at some point, each person with an addiction can come to the point where they have had enough of the craziness – and they look for answers. They may eventually look within themselves to find their own answers, to make sense of their life. Not only does the addicted person look inside, but their family and friends caught up in the maelstrom also can turn inside when they feel powerless to help their loved one.

At some point, the pleasure you seek in excessive food, alcohol, drugs, gambling, sex, shopping, or smoking ceases to be pleasurable. At some point, you acknowledge the emptiness within you that you have been trying to fill – and you admit, "What I'm doing is *not* working!"

At some point, your frustration can lead to a spiritual journey. You seek spiritual answers rather than earthly consumption to feel full. Often, when everything we've tried hasn't worked, that's when we are brought to our knees and we seek answers from a different source.

The journey to wholeness comes as a result of feeling broken. There comes a point when you look in the mirror and say, "OK. I'm ready to do it differently, because what I've tried doesn't work."

Coming to this point doesn't mean that suddenly everything changes. Yes, things change and still you have work to do: Your work is to walk away from your old ways of thinking and doing, and create a new relationship with yourself and your higher self, whatever that means to you.

To find wholeness means you see yourself as whole. This is a path of discovery, an ongoing process of coming to know yourself as the spiritual being inhabiting this "earth suit" called your body. And even when you know that you are a spiritual being, the discovering continues. It's one thing to know it intellectually, and it's quite another to live from that knowing moment-by-moment. Most of us fall somewhere on the spectrum between these two approaches: Between seeing ourselves only as a human being to living our lives knowing we are a spiritual being.

When you can see the wholeness in yourself, you can begin to see the wholeness in others, even those who seem lost in addiction. It's hard to see wholeness when someone's life is in shambles. But we are called to look beyond the shambles, the broken promises, and the self-destructive life choices. We look beyond their behavior and know this one truth: They too are whole. They too are a spiritual being in a human form. And they too are doing their best to get back to wholeness, even when it doesn't look that way.

Any time you feel less than whole, you are engaged in a spiritual journey to find the truth of your wholeness.

So how do you do that? What can you actually do to experience wholeness?

First and foremost, remember this Truth: You are not broken. You are whole. You are whole as a spirit within this body. Yes, your actions, choices, thoughts, and emotions can make you *feel* less than whole, but that doesn't mean you *are* anything less than whole. Everything in your life is meant to help you return to recognizing your wholeness.

To return to wholeness, acknowledge all sides of a situation.

Create a practice of seeing different viewpoints and other sides of the picture. See your situation from a different perspective. If you have trouble seeing anything other than your own perspective, try imagining you are someone else, someone who would see your situation from a broader viewpoint. What would they say about your situation? Just imagine it. You don't even have to know of such a person to do this. Imagine them looking at your situation and then listen to what they say. You'll be surprised and pleased with the wisdom this non-judgmental viewpoint can bring.

The next chapter, Our Balancing Act, delves more deeply into the duality of life and our ability to live with contradictions, opposites, and the paradoxes inherent in life.

You are on the path to wholeness as you begin to: Love yourself more; forgive yourself; and recognize your inherent worth and value as the person you are. You have come into this life to experience your wholeness, as you are, with the personality you have, and the "troubles" and obstacles you face. It's your soul's choice to come into this life, and it's your human choices that determine how well and fully you live.

If you have an active addict of any form in your life, or if you are actively addicted to any substance or activity yourself, remember: You signed up for this learning before you came into your body.

If the addict is someone else, know that maintaining a spiritual point of view doesn't mean that you pretend their unacceptable behavior is acceptable. It is not. Rather, walk a line, holding onto both sides of the equation. On the one side, they are a spiritual being on a journey of learning and discovery. On the other side, they are a human being making choices that adversely affect themselves and others, and it's not acceptable to be pulled into or be responsible for their drama.

Your job is to love them, see them as whole, and set healthy boundaries.

Look at your own life to see the lessons you are learning from your own type of addiction, whatever it may be. Some common lessons of addiction are:

- Commitment – Following through on your promises.
- Integrity – Keeping your word to yourself and others.
- Discipline – Strengthening your will and intention to act a certain way.

- Love – Loving yourself no matter how you continue to fall back into old destructive habits.
- Connection – Learning to be in relationship with others in healthy, real ways.
- Spiritual awareness – Perhaps most importantly, come to know yourself as the spiritual Being you are, and come into a relationship with the Source of life.

How many of these can you relate to as important in your life? They are pertinent to all of us, not just those dealing with active addiction.

Addiction is not better than, or worse than, any other path of learning. For that is what it is: A path of learning. Life can become much easier when you deal with conflicts internally, rather than turning outside yourself for comfort, love, or companionship. You *can* turn something that has been destructive and unhealthy into the fuel to live a life filled with creativity, fulfillment, and success.

10

Our Balancing Act

*"So divinely is the world organized that everyone
of us, in our place and time, is in balance with
everything else." – Johann Wolfgang von Goethe*

his world is overflowing with opposites: Dark and light,
up and down, in and out, love and hate, good and evil.
Great teachers describe the principle of "holding opposites"
using different terms, but they're all speaking about essentially the
same thing: Paradoxes, balancing, equilibration, duality, yin and yang.

You cannot have wholeness when you ignore or discount an
entire opposing point of view. That's like saying there is only light
and no dark. When we only see one side of anything in our lives,
fostering our spiritual growth and learning requires understanding
other viewpoints.

So many of us say, "I want to be whole." If this is your desire,
then realize that to embody wholeness means you need to see all
sides of a situation and balance them within yourself. This means
you learn to live with, and indeed embrace, what you perceive as
paradox and duality.

Wholeness means just that: We acknowledge the whole
situation or condition rather than just one side of it. So many
people haven't learned that they can hold opposing views at the

same time. We are taught that there's a right and wrong, good and bad, and you had better figure out which is the right and good side and hold tight to that viewpoint. We haven't been taught how to balance all viewpoints within ourselves.

So often in the midst of a tragic event, we are polarized into only seeing one side of it. We may label the event bad or evil or unfortunate. For instance, with all the mass shootings and terrorist bombings, we instinctively think of them as tragedies and judge them as "wrong." For a decent, loving, responsible human being, that judgment seems like the "right" way to look at the event. Yes, it is a tragedy, and great wrongs have befallen those affected.

But, believe it or not, *all* situations also contain the polar opposite perspective from the way you might view them. For instance, the person doing the harm to others could see his actions as right and justified. He will have a story in his mind about the reasons he wants to inflict the harm – and he believes he is right. You, on the other hand, likely think he is absolutely wrong. Just know that as strongly as you feel about your position – such as, the other side is the very face of evil itself – the other side thinks the same about his position with *equal* intensity.

For many people, this may bring a new twist to your previous perspectives. Of course you know that people have opposing views to yours, but can you even wrap your mind around this: *Both* sides are equal? Even as you read this, notice if you have the thought, "Yes, perhaps, but… My side is more right, the true right, and the other side is less than and is definitely wrong."

You, of course, think you are on the "right" side, and you will fight for what you believe is correct. Even if you don't think of yourself as a fighter, you probably do this all the time. Think about the conversations you have in your head when you're upset with someone or some situation. Admit it: You're right and they're wrong. As you look more closely and openly, however, you may get a glimpse of the situation from their perspective. You might even go so far as acknowledging your "wrongness" and the role you played in the upset. It does, after all, take two to tango, as they say; even when the two are in your own head.

A client of mine, Sheila, illustrates this perfectly. You may be able to relate to this example yourself. She was sick and tired of her husband taking everything personally and turning against her. She would make a comment or suggestion that he would interpret as, "there you go again, telling me what to do!" His confrontational attitude had become very painful for her.

In working with her, using equilibration training I learned through the Demartini Institute, she began to see how and when *she* has taken things personally throughout her own life. She had not previously acknowledged her own similar behavior. Sheila saw the benefits to her when he takes things personally, such as the opportunity for her to "mentor" him, which is a skill she values in herself. She also acknowledged the benefits to others when she is doing the same behavior.

In relationships, it's quite common to have the wish, "If only she/he were the opposite, things would be wonderful." So to bring that one-sided desire into balance, Sheila listed the drawbacks if he were to *not* take things personally. For instance, he would have more friends who would visit, and she would feel obligated to entertain them rather than having time for herself.

By examining all sides of the issue, she was able to release the painful "right and wrong" judgments and emotions. Now she giggles when she observes him taking things personally, because she sees all the sides of that behavior and no longer has polarized feelings.

Throughout your life, you get into minor disagreements with family, friends, colleagues, and even with yourself in your own mind. Are you blatant about telling others how wrong they are, or are you subtle, so that you tend to communicate in such a way that it doesn't *seem* as though you are right and they are wrong?

Notice how you respond, either out loud or just in your mind, as you watch the nightly news or read the newspaper. Do you strike out against "the other side" from what you believe? Do you talk about how "the government isn't doing it right"? Do you sign petitions against "the big companies that are to blame"?

Be honest here: The meaning you give your opinions is that you are right, as in "God is on my side." This is a really high level of rightness, isn't it? Is there any higher? Are you sure you are really this "right"?

Every four years, the United States goes through the process of electing a new president, as well as members of Congress. Most people get caught up in supporting one side or the other, Republican, Democrat, Independent, Green Party, or some other party. People also tend to prefer one candidate within their party over the others. It is usually a year or more of actively pointing fingers, blaming others, and definitely not seeing the value in the other parties' points of view. There is a decided lack of well-rounded perspectives in this process. This is not wholeness.

To be whole, to feel whole, requires that you see both sides, all sides, because there is no up without down, no dark without light, and no north without south. You may not agree with the other side, but wholeness requires that you not only acknowledge the other viewpoint, but that you also see the blessings or rightness of the opposing side.

Make no mistake, this is deep spiritual work.

The paradox of life is that opposites co-exist and co-arise with each other. For instance, people think abundance is about wealth. In truth, abundance includes scarcity, because scarcity is part of the whole. So when we push aside all thoughts of scarcity and refuse to see where we have scarcity thinking, then we are off center.

Here's a story I've heard many times. It has several variations, but the same theme. A farmer used an old horse to plow his fields. One day, the horse escaped. When the farmer's neighbors heard, they said, "Oh, that's bad luck for you." The farmer replied, "Perhaps." A while later the old horse returned with a herd of horses from the hills. His neighbors were happy for him and said, "Oh, what good luck." The farmer replied, "Perhaps." While attempting to tame one of the wild horses, the farmer's son broke his leg. The neighbors commented, "Oh, what bad luck." "Perhaps." But then soldiers came into the village to collect all the young men to fight, and the son was not able to go because of his broken leg. "Oh, what good luck." And so the story continues.

For you to return to wholeness, embrace all sides. Find gratitude and blessings in what appear to be tragedies. Recognize the downsides in what appear to be successes. And acknowledge the good in the bad, and the bad in the good. In the yin and yang symbols, part of the black is in the white and part of the white is in the black. That's what wholeness looks like.

In practical terms, how can you agree with both sides when you actually strongly disagree with the "other" side, when you see them as wrong, evil, or despicable? The good news is: You don't have to agree that they are right – but neither are they wrong. Right and wrong are subjective viewpoints, not facts. The other side thinks they are right and you are wrong. So who is right and who is wrong? The answer is, of course, neither and both: Both sides are right and wrong, and neither side is right or wrong. Both sides inherently carry within themselves equal amounts of rightness and wrongness.

So the spiritual practice becomes: Do not label either as good or bad, right or wrong, because we never know the entire picture. We can't know for sure if it's good or bad, even though we think we know.

Many people I have met who have gone through a life-threatening illness, such as cancer, say that it was the best thing that happened to them. How can that be? Well, while they were going through it, they may not have felt that way. But in looking back, after their health returned, they could acknowledge their life changed for the better. Their illness set them on a new and more desirable path of life. So was the cancer good or bad? The answer: Both.

If you are polarized in your thinking, holding deep resentment or judgment against another person, then you can now see that you are not feeling whole or centered. Your resentment and judgment take you off center to the side of the spectrum called, "I'm right and you did me wrong." Feel the effect that polarization has in your body. It's likely you will:

- Feel tense,
- Get a headache,
- Have a stomach ache,
- Create a neck ache,
- Be overly irritable,
- Endure non-stop mind chatter about what's wrong with them,
- Or any myriad of other discomforts.

Your mind and body are not at peace when you are pulled into a "me versus them" mentality.

Depending on how deeply you hold the resentment, you can do your own work to resolve your inner conflict. You may need to seek help if you're deeply entrenched in your inner battle. But you can begin on your own to calm your beastly thinking and uncomfortable feelings and return to a centered, loving place within yourself.

Balancing Opposites

Here is a spiritual practice, or an exercise, that I call "balancing opposites," which I learned in several trainings I attended, and then merged the pieces together. With this exercise, you can learn the principle of balancing opposing viewpoints, emotions, or energies at the same time.

Pick a subject where you have strong feelings against the other side: A conflict within yourself about what to do, another person's behavior, a company's policies, some atrocity, an environmental abuse, or a religious dogma.

Take a deep breath and close your eyes as you bring your attention inside yourself. Focus on your breathing for a moment, following your breath in and out as you slow down inside. Clear your mind by being aware only of your breathing.

Then bring to mind your side of the story. For example, let's say you are angry with another person because they were rude to you, and you can't get past your anger to feel loving toward them. So, feel your anger.

Look inside yourself and give your anger a size, a shape, a color, a location, and/or a feeling. Notice it in your body. Feel it clearly enough so that you could describe it to another person.

When you have your anger vividly in your mind and body, bring in the opposite. This could be feeling peaceful toward the other person, or loving, or acknowledging a past kindness. Let the opposite appear within you, also as a size, shape, color, location, and/or feeling. You don't have to logically think of the opposite; it can spontaneously appear.

Now, let both sides just co-exist within yourself. Don't do anything with them. Don't try to make the situation okay, or have one side do anything to the other side. Just watch the two sides. Be present with both. Be silent. Be observant. Be patient.

This is "balancing opposites," and you may be surprised and fascinated with what you observe occurring within you. I often have had one side start a fight with the other, or try to overpower it, or want to make itself right. I just watch. I don't take sides or try to "fix that fight within." You can do the same.

Just notice what happens as both sides are allowed to be whatever they represent. Keep breathing slowly and deeply.

For me, the bully part is the loud one, and I can hear the conversation in my mind as it screams at the other side about why it is right and why the other side is a wimp or wrong. Whatever the case, I watch and listen in my mind. I notice that the softer part is often more silent, waiting for the loud bully part to have its say. Your practice here is to give both parts enough space within you to fully express and be fully heard. You don't *do* anything, just observe.

You may become aware of your own fears and insecurities, longings and desires, strengths and weaknesses. As the two sides express themselves, they may negotiate a compromise within, or merge, or somehow change or morph into some other emotion or thought. They can become like the yin and yang, one within the other. There is no right or best outcome. It's just you coming into balance within yourself as you allow all sides of a situation to be recognized and acknowledged.

As these parts balance themselves within you, it doesn't mean you don't have opinions or viewpoints. However, it does mean that you see the bigger picture and acknowledge ways you are the same as the opposing side.

This is a deep spiritual practice and definitely is not a common approach. "They" like to take sides, to create controversy and drama, while "we" are more open-minded. If you believe this statement is true for you, there's still more work to do until you know there is no "they" and no "we."

Trust and Betrayal

I imagine you have had the experience of believing someone betrayed you, or in some way went against your wishes. It's something we all experience as part of being in relationships with others. When another person lies, deceives, betrays, or rejects you, you can be devastated and set yourself on a path of suffering.

Think back to a betrayal you experienced and notice how many times you have replayed that story in your mind. Notice how long you have held onto all the feelings you experienced because of that betrayal. Have you held on for minutes, days, months, years, or are you still holding on? How many people have you told your story to, and did they all agree with you? "Yes, that was a horrible betrayal for you. Look what it did to your life!"

What if I were to tell you, "There is no such thing as someone betraying you"? What if there is another way of perceiving what you call betrayal?

Betrayal means that someone does you wrong. You perceive it as an action against you. But consider an alternative viewpoint: What if it wasn't *against* you at all, but rather simply *for* the other person? What if they were doing what they needed to do, only acting in alignment with their personal set of subconscious belief systems, emotions, objectives, and values? Think about it. Could this have been true? Likely, yes. They were acting in their own best interests, according to what was important to them.

You, on the other hand, had expectations of how they should act. But they didn't follow *your* expectations. They may have gone back on their word to you. If so, that's about them, not you. They did what they did *for* themselves and you interpreted it as *against* you. It's a matter of perception.

Our culture loves to indulge in the "myth" of betrayal rather than seeing it for what it is: People acting according to what they value and give meaning to. Seeming betrayal is not easy to let go of, especially if you have been on the receiving end of someone's behavior that left you with unmet expectations and desires.

As a first step, be honest with yourself. Look to see: Were there any warning signs prior to the betrayal that you ignored? For example, let's say your girlfriend cheated on you. Perhaps she did that with a boyfriend prior to meeting you, but you ignored her previous behavior because you thought, "I'm different; she wouldn't do that to me." Or perhaps *you* have cheated on previous girlfriends. Are you surprised that the Universe brought it back into your life to experience the effects of your past behavior? Or perhaps you had an inkling, a knowing within you, that something was "off" in your relationship, but you didn't want to address it. We commonly avoid facing reality by brushing such feelings aside with, "It will just go away."

We are all connected energetically, thus we can tap into a greater knowing than our intellect. We are all given thoughts or bodily sensations to let us know something is going on that we need to acknowledge. If we pay attention, and take appropriate action, we can often save ourselves additional grief.

Learning from Betrayal

We can learn valuable lessons by experiencing the feeling of someone betraying us. I've had clients who experienced multiple perceived betrayals in this lifetime: In relationships, at work, and in their body becoming seriously ill. In the following paragraphs, I have combined several stories because they have similar themes.

These clients often experienced a pattern of betrayal since childhood. In fact, in going back into past lives, they found perceived betrayal there as well, which discouraged them further – until they went into the spirit world and met with their council of elders. That's when they saw that the wisdom and value of the betrayals were for their soul's growth.

As devastating to the quality of one's life as betrayal can be, it is balanced by the importance of the lessons learned. In their current life, these clients are heavily invested in helping other people heal or in some way transform their lives after tragedy or setbacks. As a result of the varying degrees and types of betrayal and deceit they suffered, these clients have learned the following lessons:

- By learning the details of being devastated, they have learned the pathways to recovery.
- They know the inner resources needed to not become bitter with themselves, with others, or with the world in general.
- They know how to develop tolerance for others' actions.
- They learned how to trust themselves and others after deceit.
- They understand the impact of public humiliation on a person and how to not let it destroy oneself.
- They realized the value of more fully discovering, knowing, and acknowledging oneself in the face of adversity.
- They have attained a deeper level of generosity as they have learned how to give back to those who have gone against them.
- They know how to give their gifts to the world in spite of loved ones working against them.
- They have learned how to gain confidence in themselves and their ability to rise back up again and again after perceived betrayals.
- They have experienced compassion for the human condition.
- They can find inner peace in times of great inner turmoil.

These are huge spiritual lessons that can take lifetimes to learn. For all my clients who felt betrayed, the purpose was always to enable them to develop qualities to bounce back and live a full life – without constantly referencing back to the betrayal.

One client experienced multiple, successive lifetimes as the victim of betrayal, until she finally learned to move through it, beyond it, and create a life based on love. Another one has spent lifetimes purposefully and deliberately walking into the betrayal snake den – to help her transform herself – and she has always gotten burned. She sees the betrayals as an opportunity to learn to rebuild her life on her own after feeling shattered. She is most proud of this skill, and she uses it to help teach others how to rebuild their lives after tragedy.

Each of these people was able to see how the betrayal was their opportunity to learn to embrace what they perceived as unacceptable. They learned that they stayed stuck in the pattern of recreating betrayal as long as they fought against it, called it wrong, and held the belief that it wasn't fair and shouldn't have happened.

Their growth occurred when they stepped away from their perception, "It's not fair," and transformed their perception to, "That's what was. It's time to move on. I can take care of myself."

Ultimately, they were all trying to learn trust. They were learning all facets of trust: To trust themselves to rebuild their lives; to pay attention to and trust their intuition; and to open their hearts to trust others again.

Think about your own life and how trust plays a role. Know that:

All of us are learning about trust in one form or another.

There are various facets to learning trust:

- Trust yourself: Listen to your intuition and take action on it, as opposed to second guessing, doubting, and not taking action.
- Trust others: Know whom to trust, and when.
- Don't trust some others: Know whom to *not* trust, and when.
- Discern: Distinguish between trusting and not trusting.

Doubt the Doubt

Doubt and skepticism play a significant role in our lives. While some people are more prone to question and doubt, others tend to more easily trust and believe in new information or ideas. If you are the analytical type, you rely heavily on your logical, rational mind to help you make decisions. You'll use facts and deductive reasoning to decide what is true and what is false or irrational. There's nothing wrong with this type of reasoning. In fact, it's very useful and important in helping you make sound, logical decisions.

Likewise, some skeptics can be very proud of their skepticism. They honor their ability to doubt or question, and they rely on facts, not feelings, for answers. In fact, healthy skepticism is an important trait for a balanced life. We all need to question and doubt rather than take everything at face value or on simple belief.

However, for some people, perhaps many people, skepticism and doubt actually get in the way of their realizing truth or making good decisions. Skepticism can cause a person to doubt and question ideas or statements that have been proven or shown to be true. Just as critics criticize because that's their nature, and that's the lens they perceive life through, so too, a skeptic can hold onto skepticism long after it's usefulness has disappeared – simply because it's become a habit for them.

Here's the problem:

We have been taught to *doubt our knowing*
and to *trust our doubt.*

Our school system and society place more relevance on our analytical, rational answers than on our inner knowing and wisdom. My point is that both are needed, both have their rightful places in our lives. When the pendulum swings too far to either side, problems occur. That's not healthy.

One important aspect of the spiritual path is balancing your logical thinking with your inner knowing. Faith is the ability to trust your inner knowing. There are things beyond your logical frame of mind that you can absolutely know and trust. But your skeptical mind doesn't allow you to trust that knowing because it's not necessarily based on facts or rational thinking. Such skepticism can lead you astray. If you find this true of you, experiment with trusting your inner knowing when it tells you something. Then look for the outcome. Was your knowing correct?

I imagine you've had the experience of driving along when you get a feeling that the car just ahead of you in the other lane is going to suddenly pull into your lane. So you instinctively back off and watch that driver carefully. Sure enough, they start to pull over into your lane but you are out of the way. Who knows how you sense that, but that advance knowing is certainly appreciated. The more you test out these senses, the more you are likely to receive and learn to trust them.

At different points in your life, you are called upon to evolve in consciousness and acknowledge that you know some things to be true.

Faith is fidelity to the insights you've gained. When you have an insight, your doubting mind may step in, making you question or think you are just making things up. My suggestion is: Be aware of your doubt. Acknowledge it and notice the role it plays in your life. How much does it interfere with or keep you from trusting your instincts? Acknowledge your doubt as one part of your experience, and, at the same time, also validate any awareness or insight you have. Let both your doubt and your awareness exist side-by-side. Hold these opposites without either one having to take over. Let yourself have doubt, if that's what you need to do. Also, let yourself have insights and inner knowing that come from a deeper place within you.

As you move along your spiritual path, you might want to have a new mantra:

I doubt my doubt…I trust my knowing.

It's a balancing act, isn't it? You learn to balance your knowing and instincts with your doubts and fears. It's all part of being human, of developing your consciousness, of growing along your path, and of paying attention to all the signs and wonders that are constantly pointing you in the direction of your highest good.

11

Inspired Living

*"When you do things from your soul, you feel
a river moving in you, a joy." – Rumi*

hat inspires you?

Think about what brings you a deep sense of well-being, joy, happiness, pride, or love when you engage in it.

What is it that you long to be, or do, or have, not in a material sense, but in your heart?

Listen to your longings.

Pay attention your discontentment.

Both are urgings from your soul. They will lead you inside yourself to discover what seems missing, unfulfilled, or just plain wrong at this time in your life. The more you are discontent, rather than filled with joy and inspiration, the more your soul is calling out to you.

If you listen to your longing and discontentment, you will be called upon to change your life. But mention "change" and people often become afraid. So they stop their inner exploration and thereby short-circuit their desires, forcing themselves back into the loop where their longings and discontentment grow louder and stronger. Such looping can continue for as long as you allow your fears to determine your actions.

One way out of this downward loop is to uncover what inspires you. Inspiration lifts us up and out of ourselves.

Rumi's quote above describes it so well. When you listen to your soul's calling, and do what you love, what inspires you, then you feel joy moving deep within you. It's a way of knowing that you are on your path, you are doing what you have come into this lifetime to do.

We all have activities that inspire us. It's inherent within us. Since you are a part of God – like a drop in the ocean of Love – then inspiration is naturally within you. It's a given.

If you are thinking, "but nothing inspires me" or "I don't know what inspires me," then you have some inner work to do. This thinking doesn't mean you aren't inspired. It just means that your inspiration is covered over by your fears, doubts, or insecurities.

And look on the other side of the coin: How are you an inspiration to other people?

You may think, "That's crazy. I don't inspire anyone and I'm certainly not inspiring or inspired." It may be that you are intimidated by the word "inspiration." I was in a weekend transformational program once when a woman was aghast at the idea that she inspired anyone. This possibility was outside her frame of reference of how she saw herself. It took some good coaching for her to recognize ways she *naturally* inspired others.

So often, we go about our day-to-day business, just being ourselves, without recognizing the influence we are having on others. For example, perhaps you naturally smile at clerks in stores or servers in restaurants. You likely will never know the influence your sincere smile had on one of those people. You may not even realize that your face radiated love with your smile. For you, it was just a polite gesture. But for them, it could be exactly what they needed at a down moment. Your smile could inspire them to smile back. And their smile could change how they felt, which changed how and what they were thinking at that moment. As their thought changed, their actions could have changed for the better.

Do you think this is a far-fetched example? It's not. It's real. I saw it happen years ago when I smiled and asked a disgruntled customer service representative, "How are you doing? You look frazzled." She responded that her daughter was in the hospital but she couldn't afford to not work. We had a brief but poignant conversation and I could see the difference in her because someone – a stranger – acknowledged her pain. A sincere smile or greeting can change someone's life. It may even stop someone from taking detrimental action in a depressed mood.

Here's another example. Perhaps you are the person others come to for advice, or they naturally pour out their hearts to you. You may be the "mother" of all the neighborhood children, giving them a big welcoming hug that tells them "you are such a wonderful child." You may even give them some good advice. Or you may be a grandparent, an aunt, or an uncle whom kids look to for comfort or fun. You may be the man everyone turns to with the request, "Can you help me with this?" or "Do you know how to fix that?"

You may have even inspired others with decisions you have made that required courage to move through your fears. You may love to travel and think nothing of going to different countries all over the world by yourself or on tours. You decide where you want to go next, and you do it. As you share your adventures on social media, you can't possibly know how inspiring you are to people sitting at home reading your posts, wishing they could do what you do. You are an inspiration just by doing what you most love to do.

The ways you inspire others don't have to be big and lofty. You don't have to be someone who changes another's world with your wisdom. Rather, you may change it for the better simply with your presence. Simply being with someone and listening without judgment can be the most inspiring thing you can do for them.

So look again at your life and see the different ways you inspire others. Studying your interactions with others isn't to pump up your ego and pride. Rather, it is to realistically acknowledge the ways you affect other people in a positive, inspiring manner.

Inspiration is your soul talking to you. It can present an idea that drops into your consciousness and excites you or makes you want to share it. You can be inspired anywhere, by anything. As you look at nature, and really take in all the beauty that surrounds you, you may become aware that beauty is inspiring. Nature is inspiring. People are inspiring. Life is inspiring. Even the world, with all its chaos and order, is inspiring.

If you feel dried up inside, void of inspiration, then I encourage you to look around for what inspires you. Breathe it in. Read books about inspiration. Listen to speakers online and on YouTube and be inspired by them. Go onto social media and begin to follow your favorite inspiring authors or speakers. Facebook is full of inspiring stories that bring tears to your eyes.

People do amazing acts of service for strangers in magnificent ways. For example, on Facebook, I saw a photo of some Hungarians standing along a road with baskets of fruits and vegetables in front of them. This food was for the refugees streaming across the Hungarian border on their way to Germany. What an inspiring notion and photo. Or another story is of the Iraqi conductor who began playing his cello at the site of a bombing in Baghdad, bringing beauty and uplifting music to a place of tragedy. Other musicians then came to the same place and, in doing what they loved, helped survivors remember there *is* good in this world.

Open your eyes and your heart to life in all its glorious moments. Yes, there is tragedy and chaos. And there is order, balance, and beauty. You may see more of one than the other. But know: It all balances out. So if you have only been seeing the dark side of life, make a daily intention to look for uplifting messages, photos, shows, and people. There truly is an equal amount, a balance between the two.

Inspired living comes from taking action on the thoughts, ideas, and inner knowing that move through you. Of course, not all thoughts and ideas are inspired, so how do you know the difference? It's much the same criteria as I presented in the chapter on Guidance and Intuition. With inspiration, you experience a positive feel, a joy in your heart, a knowing in your solar plexus, your gut instinct. It's something that moves you, often to tears or to laughter or to spontaneously putting your hand on your heart.

Acts of Service

In a coaching program in which I'm involved, in every session we are asked a simple question: What do you love? What would you love to dedicate your life to? What would bring you joy if you were to accomplish it?

I have found that when we follow our heart, we engage in acts of service to others in some form or another. Even if you think you are doing something just for yourself, it's highly likely that others will be served in some way.

For example, I know a young teenager who loves to play the trumpet. He loves to be on stage and perform. So, on several occasions, he has played his trumpet for homeless people being served dinner at a church shelter – for free. Yes, he's doing it to perform, because that gives him great joy. And, by doing what he loves, he is serving others who appreciate his music.

Each and every one of us is called in some form or other to be of service, whether to an individual, a group, the earth, animals, a country, or the world. You are here to make a positive impact on other people, in small and great ways. Studies have proven that when we genuinely help others through volunteer service, we live longer, we deal with stress better, and our body feels better as we flood it with "feel good" chemicals. Being of service to others can give your life meaning because that's the way each of us is wired.

So many people think their life purpose is a job or a career. I assure you, that's not it. Your career may help with your life purpose. But what's important to your soul is how you are acting, speaking, and influencing, no matter what you are dong.

If you feel called to be a healer, or help others transform their consciousness, then your job may be related to your purpose. But that's not necessarily true. You can be a healer, but perhaps you are really here to learn and master patience. In that case, you can learn patience in any setting, in any corporate or non-corporate job, anywhere in the world. To learn patience, your specific job is not what's important to your soul's growth – even though it can be absolutely beneficial to mankind.

A "calling" will always benefit others. So that's one way you know your soul is calling you. If you are called to a certain area of study and think, "this is just for me," then pay attention to how you will use that knowledge. Will you share it directly by talking about it, or use it to somehow further your work or career? Either way, you will benefit others. The service you provide may be direct – as in helping others transform or regain health in some capacity – or it can be indirect – by improving the situations or conditions of others.

Just know that your soul will call to you in ways you don't expect or could possibly imagine. Perhaps this new path comes to you quietly over time – maybe even since you were a child. Your calling can also unfold in you gently, urging you to take a class, read a book, or talk to a person who tells you something that piques your interest. Perhaps you have always loved to bake and now you feel called to help feed the homeless, create a cookbook, or write a blog on baking.

Your soul's calling may even be what you have been doing all along, yet you didn't recognize it was your calling. You thought you needed to do something else, or something special, rather than realizing you are already following your calling. Or one day, you may experience the sensation of the heavens opening up and you are struck with the thunderbolt thought: "This is what I have to do!" Something within you awakens and you are suddenly driven to move in that direction. You change careers, move across the country, go back to school, or take some other totally unexpected action.

Your calling will stretch your. You will learn new skills. And you will go deep inside yourself to find a wellspring of talent, wisdom, or abilities you may not have recognized you had. You will find yourself doing things you never dreamt of doing. Step by step, you are inspired to move out of your comfort zone and beyond your demons of fear, doubt, and insecurity. As you surmount these long-lived limiting beliefs, you come alive in a way you hadn't previously known. You experience the river of joy – as Rumi notes – moving through you as you walk your path.

Wayne Dyer, who devoted so much of his adult life to inspiring others and helping them transform their lives once said:

> *"When you dance, your purpose is not to get to a certain place on the floor. It's to enjoy each step along the way."*

Your soul's calling is not a destination; it's a journey – perhaps even becoming a dancing journey where you enjoy the variety of steps. You will become more and more enamored with the ideas you get, and then challenged by how much you might change and grow to fulfill your desires. It's your choice to enjoy each step of the way, or, if not all of them, at least enjoy many of the steps. You will have a sense of achievement as you surmount each hurdle. Some hurdles may seem small; others may loom large in your mind, but keep going.

Sit back for a moment, close your eyes, and let yourself remember: "How and where did I first know my calling for this lifetime?" Revisit Chapter 3, page 41, on Meaning and Purpose and do the exercise entitled "The Lifelong Thread." Look back over your life and allow the memories that first contributed to your calling to come to mind.

In my case, I took a weekend workshop on belief systems when I was 30 and I was captivated by the ideas that our thoughts actually create our lives. Something in me called me to study it more, and more, and more. I didn't start doing this work for a living until I was 48, although I never stopped studying it.

Now 35 years after that first workshop, I'm still engrossed in the work of transforming lives by assisting others in shifting their thoughts and perceptions. I never had any thought that I'd affect thousands of lives, but that's what has happened. One day at a time, year after year, I have found myself inspiring others. I've learned that it's never too early or too late to listen to your soul and be of service to others.

Your calling can come later in life. Many famous people didn't find their calling (and become famous for it) until well into their forties, fifties, sixties, and even eighties.

- Grandma Moses didn't begin painting until she was 78.
- Gandhi was 61 when he led the Salt March in India to protest the British salt tax. He walked 240 miles in 24 days, which set off the fight for Indian independence from Great Britain.
- Laura Ingalls Wilder didn't publish her first book, *Little House on the Prairie*, until she was 64.

The list goes on and on. It's never too late, or too early, to listen to what your soul is calling to you. It doesn't have to be "big and important." It's simply what your heart and soul desire. And yes, it is definitely within you. You are not the "one exception" whose soul doesn't have desires, intentions, and plans for this lifetime.

Creativity

Just as inspiration is inherently within us, because we are an extension of Source, so too is creativity part of our nature. How can it be otherwise? We are made of the same essence as That Which Created The Universe, also called God, Source, Infinite Oneness, and many other names. Since you are part of the Creator, it stands to reason that you also have creativity as part of your essence.

You may be fortunate by being blessed with artistic talent and creativity. Perhaps you ooze creativity from every fiber of your being. I have friends like this, and it's wondrous to behold their creations: Drawing, poetry, beadwork, music, gardening, baking, photography, fashion, writing, and home decorating, to name just a few areas. It's easy to see their creativity.

But what if you (like me) don't see yourself as having artistic talent? You may think you're not creative, but nothing could be further from the truth. You are creative in your own way. Perhaps you are a creative problem solver, so your creativity expresses in the ways you think up ingenious solutions or new ideas.

Possibly you are creative in how you raise your children, devising all sorts of interesting and stimulating learning possibilities for them, or creating themed birthday parties with child-enticing games and decorations.

Think about it. How do you use your creativity to relate to other people? For example, do you have an innate ability to look people in the eye and understand the deeper levels of what they are saying, or not saying? Do you naturally respond to them in ways that help them see their situation in a different light? If so, this is your creativity at work, as you figure out different scenarios to interact with other people.

You were born to create. Period. It is part and parcel of who you are. It can make you feel more alive, regardless of the level of talent you think you possess. It's not about talent and how "good" it is. Creativity is about releasing what is within you. You are meant to let it out, so do it!

If you have lost yourself in a high-stress job or chaotic family life, you may believe your creativity has dried up. In fact, creativity may be the last thing on your mind as you struggle to make ends meet or maneuver your way through a stressful situation. Rather than being the last thing, perhaps you can experiment with it being the first thing. Even if you just take a short time out from your routine to be creative, do something you enjoy. See how your body and soul react.

Dance around the house and let your body express physically. Turn up the music in your car and sing along, moving your body to the beat. Let creativity flow through you. You will be surprised what else opens up for you. If you are shut down and depressed, you are not letting the magic and mystery of life flow through you. Let your body express itself through movement and song. Draw, paint, cook, think up a new invention, or work in the garden. Do anything to get your body and energy moving. Both encourage creative juices.

You are creating every day of your life whether you realize it or not. The question you can ask yourself is this: "Do I have a plan or a vision for my life?" If you do, then you are creating by design. You are designing your life and moving toward your vision and goals, and your decisions are conscious. You can make better decisions when you actually know the direction you are headed.

Conversely, if you don't have a goal or heart's desire of what you want to create and bring to life, then you are creating your life by default. You are simply allowing each day to unfold, which leaves you dealing with whatever life presents to you. This is a very different form of creation than determining what you want to create and then moving in that direction.

Your soul speaks through your desire to make things happen, to create something new in life. It can be simple or profound. Its size is not the point. What's important is that you see yourself as the creator of your life. You are constantly creating your life experiences through your thoughts, actions, and emotions. Listen to what your heart really wants and begin to create that.

If you are already doing this, you know how good it feels! There is such a deep sense of satisfaction and well-being when you decide you want to do something that you haven't done before, and then you actually do it.

What do you want to create? What is being called forth from within for you to manifest? Whether you want to do something on your own or be part of a community effort, get going on it. Look your fears and excuses in the face and realize they are just that: fears and excuses. They are not the truth. Rather, they arise for you to move through them and beyond – so that you grow, learn, thrive, and expand your abilities, your consciousness, and your impact on the world. Go for it!

No Pocket Needed

I hope that you now have a better sense of how your soul is constantly talking to you, guiding you, giving you messages through your intuition, inspiration, creativity, desires, longings, discontentment, and through a deep sense of knowing. It's part of your spiritual path to pay attention, use your discernment, and then follow through with action.

As you step forward into the unknown, the path appears before you, one step at a time. As you trust yourself more, you expand your ability to trust yourself ever more deeply. It's a skill that grows with use. Said another way: The only way to trust yourself is to actually do it – trust yourself. Know that you are on your soul's path and just keep going, following the clues given to you from so many directions. Most especially, follow your heart because it will not lead you astray.

I started this book with the story about the moment of my father's death. I end with another story about the passing of a great and wise master teacher, Dr. Wayne Dyer. Here is an email sent on September 7, 2015, by Reid Tracy, President and CEO of Hay House Inc., and a very close friend of Wayne Dyer:

"Wayne Dyer passed away on August 30th. It seemed like a random day and a tragic loss for so many of us. But as we were preparing his obituary and information for the press release about his passing we were going through *I Can See Clearly Now*, his memoir for information to share about his life: we noticed that August 30th was in fact a very important date in Wayne's life.

August 30, 1974 was, in fact, what Wayne considered the most important day of his life. It was the day that Wayne went to the gravesite for the father he never met in Biloxi, Mississippi. After going to his father's grave, he wrote *Your Erroneous Zones* in 14 days, and his life changed forever.

So Wayne passed away exactly 41 years after the most important day of his life."

Three days before his transition, Dr. Dyer posted this message on Facebook: "I have a suit in my closet with the pocket cut out. It's a reminder to me that I won't be taking anything with me. The last one I wear won't need any pockets."

The timing and content of that post, along with the auspicious date of his transition, seem to make it clear that he was prepared to move on to his next adventure, as he called it. He lived his life well.

At face value, his "no pocket" post seems to be about not taking any material possessions with you, which is true. But think about it. It's also about energy and residue from this lifetime. He may be reminding all of us to not carry with us any resentment, non-forgiveness, grudges, or anything else that detracts from the magnificent spiritual being that each of us is. Rather, when you leave this earth, take only Love with you. Take only all that you have learned and grown through. Take only your higher consciousness and your soul's growth. Nothing else is needed on your journey home. Love will guide you home.

As you move forward in your life, dear reader, my hope and prayer is that you listen to your soul's calling, and that you leave this life with your two thumbs up, joyfully and proudly exclaiming, "I did it! I created the life I planned and wanted!"

Appendix A

Evidence of Past Lives

I have included this extra material about past lives for those who are interested in pursuing this subject further. There is also information on my website, *www.nancycanning.com*.

Belief in reincarnation is widespread. While Christianity does not endorse this belief, it is a foundational belief of Hinduism and its 850 million followers. It is part of the Sikh religion, as well as the Druse community who practice a variation of Shi'ite Islam. Belief in the cycle of rebirth is not limited to Asian and Middle Eastern religions.

Famous people throughout history have been avid believers in it, including Aristotle, Plato, Julius Caesar, Leonardo da Vinci, Shakespeare, Benjamin Franklin, Ralph Waldo Emerson, Leo Tolstoi, Henry David Thoreau, Albert Einstein, Walt Whitman, Thomas Edison, Carl Jung, and General George S. Patton, to name just a few.

Many people think that their belief in reincarnation has to be based on faith rather than on substance or evidence. Nothing could be further from the truth. If you primarily rely on logical, analytical reasoning to determine your worldview, and if you haven't researched or read much about past lives, you may be surprised to know how much research has been conducted in this area.

A Harris Poll in November 2013, based on 2,250 adults, was entitled "What People Do and Do Not Believe In." It stated that 24% of Americans believe in reincarnation, 27% aren't sure, and 49% do not believe in it. I have to wonder where that poll was taken, because location makes a significant difference in the results. If adults in California were polled regarding belief in reincarnation, it's likely the number would be higher than 24%, especially if compared with polling fundamentalist Christians in the Bible Belt in the southern United States where the number most likely would be much lower.

One of the "giants" in research on past life regression was Dr. Ian Stevenson, who passed away in 2007. In 1967, working at the University of Virginia in Charlottesville, he founded the department that conducts survival research, including near-death experiences, out-of-body experiences, visions of deathbed apparitions, after-death communication, and reincarnation. For forty years, Stevenson was in charge of researching over 2,500 cases of children from all over the world who remembered past lives. It's interesting to study children's cases because they are too young to have knowledge of many of the facts and details they report.

An article, entitled "Reincarnation: Death, Birth & Everything In Between," appeared in the Spring 2006 magazine, *What Is Enlightenment?* Author Carter Phipps writes about being struck by the sheer quantity of evidence that has been painstakingly gathered since Stevenson began his field research in the 1960s. Phipps writes:

> "I simply had no idea, prior to beginning this article, that such a formidable body of scientific research had been conducted, and at a major American university no less. Individually, the stories are striking and convincing, and many simply defy prosaic explanations. Indeed, the explanations that immediately come to mind − fraud, fantasy, faulty memories, wishful thinking on the part of the parents − do not readily apply to a significant number

of these cases. The stories have been carefully researched, and family members and friends have been interviewed. Taken as a whole, these files constitute what is probably the single best collection of evidence for reincarnation on the planet today. What may be a matter of faith for billions of people around the world has been, for the last forty years in this small office, a matter of empirical study."

When Phipps questioned whether the studies prove the case for reincarnation, Dr. Jim Tucker, a prominent researcher who took over the Division of Perceptual Studies upon Stevenson's retirement in 2002, explained that the word "proof" is not used because there is no way to scientifically test reincarnation under tight laboratory conditions where other variables can be ruled out. Ian Stevenson said that reincarnation is the best explanation, but not the only one, for the strongest cases. They provide evidence.

Proof is a mathematical term, while science provides statistical evidence. Those in the field refer to past life recall as suggestive, supportive, and evidence of lives lived prior to this current life. Past life memories in young children provides evidence that consciousness and memories do not end with death but can be brought into other lifetimes and re-accessed.

Research by Non-believers

A book I consider to be a classic, and the first book I recommend to anyone interested in reincarnation (especially to those who are skeptical), is *Many Lives, Many Masters*. It is written by Dr. Brian Weiss, a graduate of Columbia University and Yale Medical School, and Chairman of Psychiatry at the Mount Sinai Medical Center in Miami.

As a traditional psychotherapist, he did not believe in reincarnation, and was slowly drawn into that world through working with a client who had experienced anxiety, panic attacks, and phobias since childhood. Using hypnosis and past life regression, he writes about their fascinating journey of healing.

Since the introduction of this groundbreaking book in 1998, Dr. Weiss has gone on to write many more books on reincarnation and the healing that occurs from past life regression therapy work. Internationally, he speaks on past lives, appears on countless interviews, and teaches students how to do past life regression.

In the late 1960s, another researcher, Dr. Helen Wambach, began conducting a 10-year survey of past life recollections of 1,088 subjects while they were under hypnosis. She collected the information by holding full-day workshops in which she led about a dozen people on a four-stage journey. For historical accuracy, she asked specific questions about the time periods and daily lives of the people noted in the regression, including their social status, race, gender, clothing, utensils, money, eating habits, housing and other similar daily living details.

After carefully analyzing the data, Dr. Wambach concluded that the information she collected was, with respect to the historical records available to her, "amazingly accurate" – with the exception of eleven subjects. Of those eleven subjects, nine gave information that deviated only slightly from the historical time frame. Thus, only 1% of those in the study were found to be historically inaccurate.

What makes this research study even more amazing is that Dr. Wambach did not set out to prove reincarnation. Rather, she expected to debunk it. The data she collected, contrary to her own predisposition against reincarnation, convinced her of the validity of past life recall.

Carol Bowman, another past life author, was drawn into researching past lives of children when her two young children began to spontaneously recall their own past lives and were cured of their persistent phobias. In 1997 she wrote the groundbreaking book, *Children's Past Lives: How Past Life Memories Affect Your Child,* based on her research of cases in which children recalled past lives and how their current lives were affected by the recall and release.

In 2001, Bowman wrote *Return From Heaven: Beloved Relatives Reincarnated Within Your Family*, in which she explores children who reincarnate into the same family. In her research, she discovered that it was *not* wishful thinking on the part of the families to have their deceased loved ones come back to them. No, instead she found conclusive evidence of their return from the mouths of the children who had returned.

Three common questions and misconceptions:

(1) "Won't I just see myself as someone famous, which isn't real?"

The first thing many people say is, "Everybody goes back to being a king or queen or someone famous, so it's not real." Based on my past 30+ years of more than 3,000 past life psychic readings and hypnosis sessions, I can assure you that this assumption is not true. Of these 3,000 past lives, about five people claimed to have been someone well-known or famous. While some clients have reported being kings/queens/nobility, they don't report being famous.

The vast majority of clients go into lives in which they are normal, everyday people, neither famous nor infamous, neither axe murders nor saviors of the free world. They are neither Attila the Hun nor Joan of Arc. Simply put, they go to rather mundane, common lives.

(2) "How do I know I'm not making this up?"

A second common question I hear from new clients is, "How do I know I'm not just making the whole thing up?" That could be true in some cases, but there is enough scientific research and evidence to substantiate the validity of past lives. Many times clients just "know" inside themselves that it's real. They distinctly "feel" a difference between *imagination* and *past life recall*. A person may not be able to convince a skeptic of this "felt ability," and yet many past life journeys are so profound and emotional that the persons who experience them are never the same again.

There are several other ways in which a past life recall differs from imagination or wishful thinking. Imagination tends to have an aspect of fantasy or a "bigger than real life" quality. We tend to make ourselves the hero or heroine, or at least someone with noble qualities who doesn't make mistakes or poor decisions. Past life recall feels more down-to-earth. There are lives in which we're not at all proud of how we lived, and yet we see how those qualities are affecting our behaviors in this life.

When we use our imagination, since it's a story about us, we tend to make up a happy life. In past life recall, on the other hand, all kinds of events show up: Unexpected deaths of loved ones, tragedies, accidents, and unwise decisions that lead to unhappy lives – generally spot on to the issue the person is dealing with in this life. These past lives are often rather mundane, boring, hard work, "one note" types of lives, which was realistic for earlier times.

There is also a difference between *spontaneous recall,* and *facilitated regression.* In spontaneous recall, you instantly experience a memory that you immediately recognize as "a flash of knowing." You absolutely feel its truth that this was indeed you (your soul) long ago.

On the other hand, during hypnotic regression, you will tend to see your environment or scene as a still life, rather than a movie. Your inner knowing fills in answers and information, as the memories unfold. The recall may not be what you would expect or even want to see, whereas, if it were your imagination dreaming this scene up, it would tend to make the scene a good story.

In spontaneous recall you're also not actively thinking, "what's the past life?" or using your logical mind. Rather, the memory comes up from within you. It's as though you can feel it in your bones, and it may have a deep emotional component. People often cry spontaneously even before they see the upsetting scene in their mind. They also can feel deep fear, with their whole body physically shaking or hurting, as they go through a traumatic past life memory.

On the other hand, if it is your imagination, you would think about it and make changes in your story as you "make it up." With recall, there's no changing the story. The scene or knowing just appears cut out of whole cloth, as it were.

I've worked with numerous fiction writers and one of them said it best, when I questioned whether she felt she had made up her past life: "Hell no, I write way better than that!"

(3) "Why even pay attention to past lives? What good does it do?"

One of the many benefits is to learn why you are here this lifetime. By looking at your past lives, you can better understand your current one. As an example, if you tend to be impatient or self-absorbed, somewhat indifferent to the needs of others, then your work this lifetime may be to foster patience and compassion in your life. Although these behaviors may not come easily to you, deep within, your soul embodies the ability to be patient and kind.

If you do a past life regression, it may lead you to a lifetime where you were impatient and self-absorbed – and you didn't change at all. Or perhaps you would go to the opposite type of life in which your personality and lifestyle made it "easy" for you to be patient and kind. Briefly experiencing either possible past life can affect how you see yourself now. In this lifetime, the lesson you perhaps came in to learn is to discipline your personality traits of impatience and indifference. Listening to your soul's calling can help you. As you realize the bigger picture of who you are, who you have been, and why you are here now, you *can* change your self-concept and behaviors.

Rather than distancing yourself from those issues, there is another way to look at them. The issues that seem to be your nemesis through life are not your enemy. They are actually showing you your life lessons for this lifetime. By dealing directly with your life events, you grow spiritually, rather than feeling victimized by life. You can learn and grow or you can carry the sense of being punished. That's called free will. Either way, you've chosen to incarnate to learn lessons through the events of your life.

You gain inner power by looking at the bigger picture of who you are and why you're here. It's neither easy nor for the faint of heart. It takes courage to face yourself. When you see yourself from the spiritual viewpoint, you begin to understand more deeply. You can begin to have admiration for who you are and what you've chosen to come in to learn. You can become compassionate with yourself for how you're doing this lifetime. Chances are, if you've read this book, then you're already on your spiritual path and already growing spiritually, because at least you have the level of consciousness to reach into your soul world for answers to the age-old questions: Who am I and why am I here?

Your soul's calling you to remember.

Appendix B

Additional Resources To Help You on Your Spiritual Path

*N*ow that you've finished reading *Your Soul's Calling*, you may be wondering, "How can I put this information to work in *my* life?" Nancy Canning has helped thousands of people on their spiritual path to realize their life purpose and release their limiting subconscious beliefs that hold them back from living fulfilling and soul-satisfying lives.

Here are ways in which you can use my expertise to delve more deeply into your own soul's journey:

Life Purpose Regression – While in a hypnotic trance, you follow the theme of your life purpose, starting with childhood and moving forward throughout your life. You don't have to know your life purpose consciously before you begin, as it reveals itself through the memories you spontaneously recall. This is a fascinating 75-minute journey that shows you to see how much you have actually been "on track" with your life purpose, perhaps without even realizing it.

Past Life Regression – In this hypnosis session you go back to a past life having a significant impact on your current life. You move through the life, the death (no pain), and then from the soul state look back to see what lessons you came in to learn, how you did, and how that life is impacting you now. At that point, we do healing and release work as needed. It's a 90-minute session, often very therapeutic as well as fascinating.

Life-Between-Lives Spiritual Regression – This 4-hour session utilizes deep hypnosis to gently move you into a super-conscious state where you can access memories of your time in the afterlife. You can view an hour-long interview with Bob Olson about the session on my website listed below. This session is based on the book, *Journey of Souls* by Michael Newton, although your session will be quite different than the book. People do this session to remember their life purpose this lifetime, learn how they're doing, who they are as a spirit, visit with loved ones who have departed, remember why they chose their family, and so much more.

Transforming Limiting Belief Systems – This 90-minute hypnosis session takes you back to the root cause (in this lifetime) of a belief that creates a limiting pattern or issue in your life. You are led through a simple process to discern how, when, and why the belief was formed, and why it is still in your life as an adult. You then are facilitated to release the belief and be free of that subconscious programming. You will typically work on two to four beliefs in one session.

Picture Your Life – This extraordinary session enables you to access your deepest desires for what needs to happen in the coming years in order to not have any regrets at the end of your life. Utilizing a meditative state and colored pens, you create a picture that acts as a compass to help you navigate the rest of your life and make decisions that are in line with your heart's deepest desires.

The Demartini Method® – I am a Trained Demartini Method® Facilitator, a method developed by Dr. John Demartini. It is a scientific process that balances perceptions and emotions. It is used professionally by many psychologists, psychiatrists, social workers, educators, consultants, and health professionals across the world. The Demartini Method® is a tool with a thousand uses for empowering and inspiring life, and its applications include reducing stress, resolving conflict, and creating new perspectives and paradigms for life. It is not hypnosis; rather you balance and release the emotional charge and energy trapped in an unresolved or troublesome issue. The outcome is a sense of deep peace and love.

All of these individual sessions can be done in person in Cape Cod, MA or by phone or Skype, except for the Life-Between-Lives session that is only done using Skype or in person. Some clients prefer the phone or Skype work because they can remain resting in their own home after the session, taking time to process all they have just experienced.

As an experienced and enthusiastic international *speaker* and *teacher*, I regularly teach past life regression workshops in the Cape Cod, MA area and am available for travel.

I also teach various classes via phone and online technology, based on my books and other transformational subjects. Attendees consistently report that their lives have changed significantly as a result of spending just a few class hours with me.

I am available for keynote speaking and facilitating transformational exercises at conferences, workshops, retreats, and gatherings, large or small. I also enjoy doing interviews on past lives, the afterlife, transforming belief systems, the mind-body connection, and the soul's journey.

You can follow me on Facebook, *https://www.facebook.com/nancy.canning.9* or *https://www.facebook.com/NancyCanningHypnotherapy* and on twitter @NCanning.

On my website, listed below, I offer free emails series on "How your past lives are impacting you" and "Discovering your life purpose." Each series is 7 short emails, arriving every couple of days over two weeks' duration. They provide insights and information, as well as leading you into your own inner knowing.

Visit my website *www.nancycanning.com* now to learn more about these resources, plus upcoming workshops, classes, and talks.

Books by Nancy Canning:

Your Soul's Calling: Answering the Question, "Why Am I Here?"
Your Life's Calling: Getting Unstuck and Fulfilling Your Life Purpose
Past to Present: How Your Past Lives Are Impacting You Now
Co-Author: *Inspiration Bible: The Unseen Force Transforming Lives Worldwide*

CDs – available on author's website *www.nancycanning.com* as download or physical CD:
Past Life Regression
Relax Now
CDs to help you transform your limiting belief systems:

Transform "I'm Not Loveable"
Transform "I'm Not Worthy, Don't Deserve"
Transform "I Worry, Doubt, Don't Trust"
Transform "I'm Stuck/Procrastinate"
Transform "I'm Not Enough"
Transform Your Finances
Transform Your Self-Image
Transform Your Self-Confidence
Transform To Your Ideal Weight
Transform Your Eating Habits
Change Any Belief

About the Author

Nancy Canning has worked with thousands of clients since 1980, helping them transform and improve the quality of their lives. She loves her work and feels honored to be part of the healing journey of so many people, from so many places around the world, including: United States, Canada, England, Ireland, Sweden, Denmark, Netherlands, Belgium, France, Spain, Portugal, Columbia, Mexico, Egypt, China, Vietnam, Japan, Australia, South Africa, and the Philippines.

She has her Master's Degree in counseling psychology, is a certified clinical hypnotherapist, international workshop facilitator, engaging teacher, trained psychic, and is certified in past lives and journeys into the afterlife.

She is the author of *Your Life's Calling: Getting Unstuck and Fulfilling Your Life Lessons*, in which you learn how your limiting belief systems were formed, what keeps you stuck in unhealthy and unproductive patterns, and how to release the beliefs and move forward into a life that serves your highest good. *Past to Present: How Your Past Lives Are Impacting You* is her mini-book that helps people understand how their previous lives still influence them today. It's an eye-opening read. She is also a co-author of *Inspiration Bible: The Unseen Force Transforming Lives Worldwide*.

She has two more books percolating within her, coming into physical manifestation in 2016 and beyond. In her next book, she will collaborate with three highly esteemed colleagues whose expertise in mind-body-spirit she highly values. The intent of all her work is to help people live a life worthy of their dreams and their soul's purpose.

Nancy offers the unique perspective of how one's past lives, in between lives, and this life all combine to create one's life lessons and purpose. She offers various free email series on her web site, as well as notices about special events and upcoming classes.

Nancy offers private sessions in person in Cape Cod, MA, on the phone, and via Skype. Visit her web site, *www.NancyCanning.com*, for details on all her offerings and to arrange a session.

CPSIA information can be obtained
at www.ICGtesting.com
Printed in the USA
FFOW01n1320061115
18341FF